So Long, Cowboys
of the Open Range

"Kid Amby" Cheney, at 16, cowboy of the open range. *Photo by Dan Dutro at Fort Benton, 1890.*

So Long, Cowboys of the Open Range

Truman McGiffin Cheney
with Roberta Carkeek Cheney

Other books by Dr. Truman M. Cheney
    Ranching in the Shadow of Wolf Butte

Books by Roberta Carkeek Cheney
    Big Missouri Winter Count
    Hans Kleiber, Artist of the Big Horns, co-author with Emmie
        Mygatt (Cowboy Hall of Fame award "Best Western Art
        Book of 1976")
    Music, Saddles and Flapjacks
    Names on the Face of Montana (now in fourth printing)
    This Wyoming—Listen, co-editor with Emmie Mygatt
    Women Who Made The West, editor, contributor, published
        by Doubleday and Avon.
    Your Personal Writers Workshop

Cover painting:
    Men of the Open Range, by Charles M. Russell, Mackay
        Collection, Montana Historical Society, Helena.

First Printing 1990
Second Printing 1991
Third Printing 1993
Fourth Printing 1995

Library of Congress Catalog Card Number 90-91858
ISBN 1-56044-048-1

Design by Laurie Gigette Gould

Publishing Consultant:
Falcon Press Publishing Co., Inc.,
Helena and Billings, Montana

ACKNOWLEDGEMENTS

An especial thank you to my wife, Roberta Cheney, for the professional assistance and the many hours she spent revising, editing, and typing this manuscript. I am grateful to our daughters, Dr. Maureen Curnow and Karen Cheney Chapman, for their thorough proofreading and suggestions, and to Dr. Robert Gunderson and his late father, Carl Gunderson, for help with pictures. I appreciate the fact that my brothers, LeRoy, Charles, William, Bernard, Ambrose, and Thomas, and my sister, May, listened to the many stories our father told of early open range days and helped me remember them. I am grateful for the first-hand background information from my father and mother and for technical critique by my son, Larry Cheney, who is a modern-day expert on cattle.

DEDICATION

In tribute to the cowboys of the open range who brought national and international fame for all cowboys. In grateful dedication to my Dad, Kid Amby Cheney, and my Mother, Elizabeth McGiffin Cheney, pioneers who lived realistically in that era that has now come to be romanticized in books and movies.

PREFACE

"Kid Amby" Cheney was a cowboy of the Montana open range cattle industry, who arrived in the Judith Basin at age fourteen in 1888, during the height of that era. He became a top-hand and "rep" with two major cattle pools—the Judith Basin Pool and the Bearpaw Pool. After fourteen years with those outfits, he turned to jerk-line freighting and then settled on a ranch of his own, married, and raised a family of seven sons and one daughter. In 1963 he was elected Honorary President of the Montana Cowboys Association, was featured in a *Life* magazine article, and later was elected to the Cowboy Hall of Fame in Oklahoma City.

It was Kid Amby's stories that provided the core material for this book's description of the harsh and humorous realities of the open range cowboy's life.

From Kid Amby, the authors heard first-hand about the "Lousy Seven Bunch" and individual cowboys such as Doc Nelson, Con Price, Teddy Blue Abbott, Charlie Russell, the outlaw Kid Curry, and the preacher, Brother Van. From him, too, we learned about a cowboy's gear and his daily work (and fun) in the roundup camps.

Amby's accounts have been rounded out with material from other personal interviews and from published and unpublished material. Abbott's and Price's own works also furnished some details. A number of accounts came directly from the writings of Amby's wife, Elizabeth McGiffin Cheney. To her we are particularly indebted for the verbatim report of the reunion of the "Three Old Cowboys."

As a son of Kid Amby, I listened to my father's songs and stories both serious and humorous. During Amby's later years, we wrote down these accounts as Amby retold and thus relived those years on the open range.

Truman McGiffin Cheney, Author

and

Roberta Carkeek Cheney, Editor

CONTENTS

* In addition to the Judith Basin and Bearpaw cattle pools material, the text includes data on the Shonkin, Moccasin, D.H.S., Square, Circle Diamond, Circle C, Chestnut Valley, Two Dot, and the '79 cattle pools.

Some of the 45 brands of the Judith Basin Pool and the Bearpaw Pool

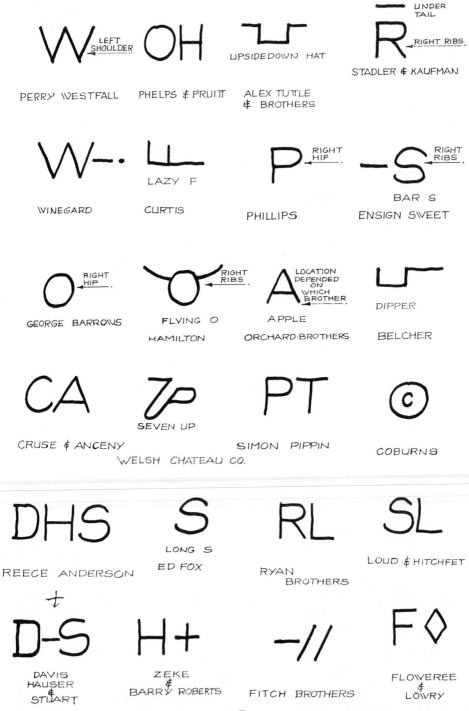

W LEFT SHOULDER

PERRY WESTFALL

OH

PHELPS & PRUITT

⊔ UPSIDEDOWN HAT

ALEX TUTTLE & BROTHERS

R UNDER TAIL — RIGHT RIBS

STADLER & KAUFMAN

W—·

WINEGARD

⊔ LAZY F

CURTIS

P RIGHT HIP

PHILLIPS

—S RIGHT RIBS

BAR S

ENSIGN SWEET

O RIGHT HIP

GEORGE BARROWS

FLYING O

HAMILTON

A LOCATION DEPENDED ON WHICH BROTHER

APPLE

ORCHARD·BROTHERS

⊔ DIPPER

BELCHER

CA

CRUSE & ANCENY

7P SEVEN UP

WELSH CHATEAU CO.

PT

SIMON PIPPIN

©

COBURNS

DHS

REECE ANDERSON

S LONG S

ED FOX

RL

RYAN BROTHERS

SL

LOUD & HITCHFET

D-S

DAVIS HAUSER & STUART

H+

ZEKE & BARRY ROBERTS

-//

FITCH BROTHERS

F◊

FLOWEREE & LOWRY

Brands from other cattle pools and owners.

7-77 ¢ 79   □   TL

SQUARE OUTFIT

JOHN T. MURPHY   MILLNER   MAC NAMAR & BROADWATER

HORSESHOE BAR   LAZY K Y   CIRCLE DIAMOND   HORSE BRAND.

T. C. POWERS   CON PRICE CHARLIE RUSSEL   BLOOM CATTLE CO.   GOVERNOR TOOLE CON PRICE CHARLIE RUSSELL

          OTO   ⟂

CIRCLE O BAR   QUARTER CIRCLE V   RANDALL   ANCHOR T

STEVENS   WILLISON   AMOS STOREY

     5T

MILL IRON   LAZY B   HASH KNIFE

COLONEL SIMPSON   LU BARLOW   COLONEL SIMPSON   SAND & TAYLOR

NL

Mᶜ NAMARA & MARLOW

Songs of the Open Range

Chorus is one Kid Amby often sang. Verses written by Truman Cheney and dedicated to Amby, one of the real cowboys of the open range days in Montana.

A Real Cowboy

Oh, the cowboy's life is a lonesome one
As he rides "trail herd" in the blazing sun.
He's covered with dust and his throat is dry,
And his voice is shrill and you hear him cry:

> CHORUS
> Old cow eatin' in the grass, see here old cow,
> I done come along and caught you with your calf.
> Get on the trail with your calf behind
> Or my horse and rope will swing you in line.
> Holading, Holading, Hol —a —ding.

His clothes are wet and his boots are, too,
As he often sleeps in the rain and the dew.
He gets up early to beat the heel flies,
To the herd of cattle, and then he cries:

> CHORUS

His food is good and his coffee's strong,
And he eats his lunch as he rides along
On a "roundup circle" most every day
You can hear him singin' as he rides away:

> CHORUS

He can winter a slicker and summer a girl,
And he seldom loses this frontier pearl
Even though he's gone on the roundup trail.
He's a singin' this song as he hopes for mail:

> CHORUS

He can rope and throw a six-year old steer,
Tie a cotton wood pole to each horn by the ear
And as this steer heads towards the herd,
He sashays out a singin' these words:

> CHORUS

He can catch his horse in a rope corral,
Never swingin' or missin' in many a spell,
Throws his saddle on and away he goes,
Singin' and ridin' where - only he knows:

> CHORUS

Old J. B.

First stanza is one Amby used to sing. Other stanzas were written by Truman
M. Cheney.

Wake up in the morning
When the dew is on the ground,
Saddle up old J.B. and watch him Hog Around,
Hog around, hog around.

Climb up on old J.B.
Pull his head up high,
Get a little shaking up
As J.B. hits the sky.

Soon old J.B. straightens out
And we're heading toward the herd.
He's still a little goosey
And a steppin' like a bird.

Cuttin' out the beef herd,
Old J.B.'s on his toes.
Never have to say a word,
Just follow where he goes.

Riding back to supper
Old J.B.'s going strong.
When I pull the saddle off,
He's at it again—Hog Around,
Hog around, hog around.

The following two songs were often sung by Kid Amby:

The Roundup Cook's Pie

Oh, they sat the pie out on the table that night.
Sure, it looked like a ship without sails,
Whilst Mulligan mended a hole in the lid
With a hammer and two or three nails.

Sure, it looked very nice
So I asked for a slice.
For I eat when I'm hungry
And drink when I'm dry.
You can say what you please,
But I've been in a daze
Since I tackled Old Mulligan's pies.

(Dedicated to Frank Graham, Tom Tomato (Matsumato), Big Nose George, Greasy Tom, Mulligan, and all the other roundup cooks.)

An Old-Time Cowgirl

I once roped a steer, but I fell.
Fell from my pony with an ear-piercing yell.
Fell with a lariat fast to my wrist,
Fell to be dragged through the grass wet with mist.
Bumping, rolling, and gruntin' I went,
A full mile a minute or I don't want a cent.
The grass and the gravel yanked the hide from my nose
And ruined a pair of my forty-cent hose.
Even my bustle was throwed out of gear
By the frolicksome pranks of that beautiful steer.

Oh, the steer, beautiful steer
With long, shiny horns at the base of each ear.
With the quick fearless eye and tapering tail
That would snap like a whip through the maddening gale.
Bellowing, roaring, thundering along
Filling the air with hysterical song
'Til the rumble from its lung laden pitch
Scared timid jackrabbits and wolves into fits. Oh, to me
    there's nothing on earth half so dear
As the long horned, slim bodied Texican steer.

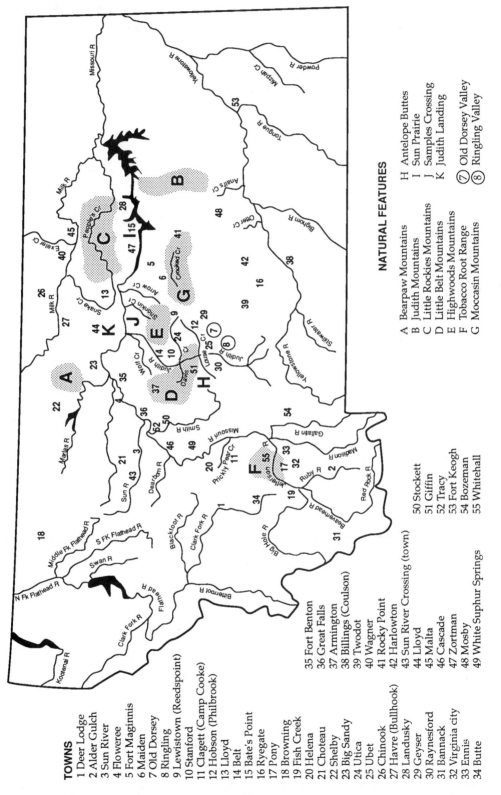

TOWNS

1 Deer Lodge
2 Alder Gulch
3 Sun River
4 Floweree
5 Fort Maginnis
6 Maiden
7 Old Dorsey
8 Ringling
9 Lewistown (Reedspoint)
10 Stanford
11 Clagett (Camp Cooke)
12 Hobson (Philbrook)
13 Lloyd
14 Belt
15 Bate's Point
16 Ryegate
17 Pony
18 Browning
19 Fish Creek
20 Helena
21 Choteau
22 Shelby
23 Big Sandy
24 Utica
25 Ubet
26 Chinook
27 Havre (Bullhook)
28 Landusky
29 Geyser
30 Raynesford
31 Bannack
32 Virginia city
33 Ennis
34 Butte
35 Fort Benton
36 Great Falls
37 Armington
38 Billings (Coulson)
39 Twodot
40 Wagner
41 Rocky Point
42 Harlowton
43 Sun River Crossing (town)
44 Lloyd
45 Malta
46 Cascade
47 Zortman
48 Mosby
49 White Suphur Springs
50 Stockett
51 Giffin
52 Tracy
53 Fort Keogh
54 Bozeman
55 Whitehall

NATURAL FEATURES

A Bearpaw Mountains
B Judith Mountains
C Little Rockies Mountains
D Little Belt Mountains
E Highwoods Mountains
F Tobacco Root Range
G Moccasin Mountains
H Antelope Buttes
I Sun Prairie
J Samples Crossing
K Judith Landing
⑦ Old Dorsey Valley
⑧ Ringling Valley

CATTLE COME NORTH
CHAPTER ONE

The era of the open range and big cattle roundups in Montana has been much publicized and glamorized in history and fiction as well as on television and in the movies. Actually, it was only a brief and transient period. It began in the mid 1870's, when great herds of "long horns" were driven up the trails from Texas and Oklahoma to graze on the open ranges that had once sustained vast herds of buffalo. Other cattle were driven over from Oregon. The Montana open range cattle industry flourished in the 1880's and was closed by 1900—with the influx of homesteaders and barbed wire.

Kid Amby Cheney, his fellow cowboys, and the big cattle pools were the reality of that open range era.

The legend has survived because "History is here, Western history, and it beats in the blood; and the visitor (or the reader) knows that there is no past; the past is now. We are captivated by sheer adventure, by the rediscovery of adventure, by the hard simplicities of loneliness, privation, danger, the elemental contests of man versus nature and man versus man. We are caught up in admiration for the men who went before, as courageous and hardy as we wish to be and never can or shall be."[1]

Actually, the beginnings of the cattle industry in Montana were humble. It is said that the first cattle in Montana were four cows and two bulls brought in by Charles Larpenteur, and by the time his party reached the mouth of the Yellowstone on September 3, 1833, his herd was down to two cows and one bull. The first cattle to come into Montana that gave rise to permanent herds were those trailed from Oregon to the western part of the state by Catholic priests in 1842.

The good "Black Robes" like Father DeSmet and Father Ravalli hoped that the western Indians could be taught to raise their own food. In 1846, St. Mary's Mission reported a herd of forty cattle, and DeSmet hoped that the Flatheads would not have to cross the Rockies and war with other tribes for buffalo. In 1860, John Owen took over the Mission buildings and brought in 300 head of cattle.

Left: Conrad Kohrs, early day cattle man and ranch owner in the Deer Lodge Valley. Right: Augusta Kohrs worked hard as a pioneer wife and added a bit of culture in the untamed land. *Photos courtesy of Grant-Kohrs Ranch National Historic Site.*

Cattle ranches were developed in the rich Deer Lodge Valley, and in 1862, the discovery of gold at Grasshopper Creek near Bannack created a big demand for meat. Conrad Kohrs, who was to become one of the important cattlemen of Montana, began by working in a butcher shop in Bannack. The opportunity to buy the shop came when the owner had difficulty with Sheriff Henry Plummer and left the area very suddenly. Kohrs soon arranged to buy worn-out work cattle from the covered wagon pioneers and trade them in Deer Lodge for fat animals. He moved to a butcher shop in Helena and began also to stock a ranch with the emaciated trail animals. Kohrs purchased the Johnny Grant ranch near Deer Lodge, which at one time ran 2,000 head of cattle. He formed a partnership with John Bielenberg, and they brought in 1,500 head of cattle from California.

Most of the supplies for the gold camps at Bannack, Alder Gulch, and even Helena were freighted from Utah by "bull teams" in the very early days. The animals, thin and worn out by the time they reached Montana, were turned out to graze and by spring were in good condition. They were the beginning of several herds.

Among the prospectors who saw more future in the cattle business were James and Granville Stuart. Granville was to become another of the powerful cattlemen. It was said that, at one time, Johnny Grant had 4,000 head of cattle and 2,000 horses. He supplied meat for the thousands of prospectors who rushed into Montana in the 1860's. Johnny was well-known in Montana.

Johnny Grant, one of the first successful cattlemen in Montana.
Photo courtesy of Montana Historical Society

The very first sign board in Montana was a rough-hewn board at the confluence of the Beaverhead River and Rattlesnake Creek with the messages daubed in axle grease. On one side:

Tu grass Hop Per digins
30 myle
Kepe the trale nex the bluffs

And on the other side:

To Jonni Grants
one Hundred & twenti myle

Another phase of the introduction of cattle into Montana were the Texas trail drives. As early as 1866, Nelson Story drove 600 head of Texas longhorns into the Gallatin Valley from Fort Worth. In 1863, he had come to Montana for the gold rush. Story stayed in Virginia City and worked with the Vigilantes in eliminating the stagecoach robbers. He also struck it rich in Alder Gulch and used his money to buy the cattle in Texas. His 1866 drive was one of the first and most hazardous of the trail drives, as he came by way of what was later to be known as the "Bloody Bozeman." He managed to evade most of the Indian toll collectors, forded swollen streams and rivers, and fought off Indian attacks. His twenty-seven men were armed with the new Remington rapid-fire breech loaders. For protection, they drove the cattle by night and corralled them by day.

Nelson Story, who in 1866 trailed 600 head of longhorn cattle from Ft. Worth, Texas, to Bozeman, Montana. *Photo courtesy of the Museum of the Rockies, Bozeman.*

With only one man killed and two injured, he reached the Gallatin Valley in December, completing the first drive over the Bozeman Trail.

In 1869, Myron Jeffers brought a thousand head of cattle up the Texas trail to Montana Territory and sold them at Bannack. In 1870, he trailed another herd into Montana and again sold them at Bannack. He trailed a third herd from Texas in 1871 consisting of 1,894 head of cattle and thirty-seven horses that were all branded on the road. This herd was used to stock his cattle ranch in the Madison Valley. In 1881, Jeffers, Ed Maynard, and Burton Jeffers formed a cattle pool and leased land on the Yellowstone. This cattle pool was dissolved in the early 1890s; the herd had been sold soon after the bad winter of 1886-7. In recognition of his trail drives, the cattle pool, and his early ranching, Myron Jeffers was elected to the Cowboy Hall of Fame in 1961.

The trail drives bringing stock into the Powder River country in southeastern Montana began in 1870. The trail used then was longer but less dangerous than the Bozeman Trail, and the Indians were becoming a little more accepting of these invasions. In 1871, Robert Ford and Thomas Dunn took a thousand head of cattle into the Sun River Valley in north-central Montana. Then, in 1873, Conrad Kohrs and John Bielenberg added to their herds by trailing over 3,000 head of cattle into that valley where they met the Texas trail herds of Dan Floweree. These herds from the Sun River area were slowly pushed eastward to eventually mingle with the forerunners and neighboring outfits of the Bearpaw Pool and pushed to the south in 1881, where Kohrs and Bielenberg later became major owners in the Judith Basin Pool. The Texas trail drives added thousands of new cattle to Montana's ranges. They had often been driven by Texas cowboys who usually headed back home after one winter in Montana. Some of them made many trips, but only a few stayed to become cowboys or cattlemen in Montana. The local open range cowboys learned a lot from the Texans.

These incoming herds needed increasingly larger grazing areas, and owners began to move their cattle into the open ranges like the Judith Basin in central Montana.

There was abundant grass in the Judith Basin because trappers and hide hunters had almost exterminated the beaver, buffalo, and most of the deer and antelope that had formerly foraged there. In 1881, cattlemen from southwestern Montana began to send their herds to the Judith Basin. There were no fences and those herds mingled with the smaller ones of ranchers in the Basin. The owners of these big herds stayed in Butte, or Helena, or Deer Lodge to run their other businesses, so they sent a manager or trail boss and cowboys to care for the stock. It soon became apparent that any separation of the herds for individual care was impossible and that pooling resources and workers was the only solution. They all had the same problems: branding new calves; shipping beef cattle; holding cattle on a given range; what to do when their cattle spread to ranges of other outfits; how much control the cattle would need in the winter;

Myron D. Jeffers who trailed a thousand head of longhorns from Texas in 1869, and in 1870 brought in another thousand head to sell in Bannack, Montana. In 1871 he trailed 1,894 head of cattle from Texas, branding them on the way. With these he established his own herd. His crew of 14 riders, a cook, and cook's helper took seven months for the 1871 trip. His Yellowstone River Cattle Pool started in the late 80s, ran into losses in the winter of '87-'88, and he sold out in 1891. *Photo courtesy of Montana Historical Society, Helena.*

how many cowboys and foremen would be needed; delineating their range borders; and dealing with the problem of cattle rustlers.

The owners were good businessmen, and they soon saw that an organized cattle pool was needed. The Judith Cattle Company had been formed in 1878, so they had valuable experience in handling cattle in a small pool. Thus, the larger Judith Basin Pool was developed in about 1885. The absentee owners and the ranchers selected a rancher-owner named Tuttle to be the first foreman of the pool.

The cattle owners of the Judith Basin Pool had regular meetings to discuss policies and problems, hire competent foremen, and decide on the number of cowboys needed—usually thirty or forty. They also determined the number of "reps" or representatives to send to the neighboring pools such as the Shonkin, Moccasin, or D.H.S. pools. They chose leaders for each of their four "outfits" and decided on new pool members. The foreman and top cowhands made branding plans and decided with the owners when and where the beef cattle should be shipped. Many on-the-spot decisions had to be made by the foreman and local owners—with advice from the top cowhands. There were always owners around when the calves and mavericks were branded and when the steers and dry cows were rounded up for shipping.

Other cattle pools were organized in much the same manner as the one in the Judith Basin and were an important part of the cattle industry in Montana until around the turn of the century. Kid Amby, Con Price, Charlie Russell, and many other cowboys got their start working for the Judith Basin Pool, and their experiences are representative of the life of the open range cowboys in Montana.

References:
1 Guthrie, A. B., "The Meaning of the West," *Life* magazine, April 13, 1959. (Reprinted in *Roundup*, Western Writers of America, Jan. 1988.)

THE GEAR AND SKILLS OF THE OPEN RANGE COWBOY
CHAPTER TWO

The working cowboys of this brief but romantic period in Montana history cannot be imitated with any success. "They belong to a breed which is as distinctive as the mustang horse and the longhorn steer."[1] These cowboys of Montana's open range were a composite of the cowboys from Texas, Arizona, Oklahoma, Wyoming, and any state along the trail where the herds came through and often picked up additional or replacement cowboys. Their influence is seen in such adaptations as chaps (chaparejos), lariats or ropes, and tapaderos or stirrup covers, and in calling the cattle "dogies." There was a skill to be learned in night guarding that included singing to the restless animals to calm them. There were variations in handling trail herds, beef herds, or those brought in for branding.

Today, boys and girls, mature men and women, as well as modern cowboys, imitate the open range cowboy and pay homage to him by wearing hats, boots, neckerchiefs, fancy shirts, and sometimes even chaps, spurs, or leather wristcuffs.

Those original cowboys were different from the cowboys, cowhands, and bronc fighters of today. The men of the open range were rough and tough characters who could single-handedly rope and tie a six-year-old steer, tie a pole to his horns so he couldn't go back into the brush, and get him back into the herd. Those cowboys could, and often did, sleep under the stars with a saddle for a pillow and a saddle blanket for a cover. They could rope horses in a rope corral without swinging a loop—just by dabbing the rope around the animal's neck or front-footing him if he was hard to handle. They swam two thousand cows, calves, and yearlings across the Missouri River or the Yellowstone in the high water of spring. They knew how to stop a stampeding herd of cattle and would risk their lives to do so. Wolves, which no longer had buffalo for food, preyed on the cattle herds, so the cowboys learned to rope them, too.

The cowboy had to be content with only a bed-roll for a home and a string of eight or ten horses as permanent companions.

Montana's open range cowboys varied in size from Baldy Buck's 320 pounds on down to Humpy Jack Davis, the orphan, who was 5' 2'' tall and probably didn't weigh a hundred pounds, but became one of the best "reps" on the roundups of north-central Montana because he could quickly spot any brand belonging to his pool. Then there was Long George Francis, who was 6'6'' tall.

There were men said to have notches in their guns like Kid Curry and his brother, Johnny; Charles Bowlegs and Bob, Will, and Wallace Coburn of the Circle C; and Long Henry of the Square outfit. There were ropers like Kid Amby Cheney and Wild Bill Sutter, who could work all day at a spring branding roundup and never miss a loop. Amby and one of his buddies were experts at the backhand loop, which always picked up both hind legs of a calf.

There were those who "died with their boots on" like Johnny Curry and Tom Starr, or the cowboys who drowned on the soft spring ice of the Missouri River trying to get to Fort Benton for a good time with the girls and liquor.

There were those who died on the job like Al Malison, who was thrown by a bronc and kicked in the legs and head so severely that he was taken to the hospital in Fort Benton where he died. Tom (Ed) Starr was shot while he was bending over to tie the picket rope on his horse, and Timberline was trampled to death by a stampede of beef steers. Add to these, the roundup cook, Mitchell, who was shot by a cowboy named "Pecos" who had come from the Rustlers War in Wyoming, and Charlie Bowlegs, who was shot in the back of the head by a man he had powder-burned in a previous shoot-out.

Who can match Con Price, Charlie Carthrae, and Doc Nelson, who rode the rough strings for many different outfits, or Kid Amby Cheney, who roped calves for two days straight at the King ranch near Lewistown and at the age of eighty-four roped 400 calves in one day?

The cowboy wasn't much for possessions; his nomadic life precluded that. Some good horses, a saddle, bridle, and lariat and a few clothes rolled up in a couple of soogans carried him through the season. Except for his hat—a good Stetson was an absolute necessity and its uses were many.

These open range cowboys used their hat to protect their heads from the sun, wind, rain, and cold. They used it, too, for dipping drinking water from a small stream or pool, or to water their horses. They used that Stetson to fan a bucking horse that they were "forking." Held in one hand, a hat helped the rider balance himself on a bucking horse. Put over a cowboy's face, the hat kept his head warm and the sun or campfire smoke out of his eyes. Used as a basket, it could hold flowers for his girlfriend or eggs that he might find. When he dressed up to go out on the town, his hat was the crowning touch for a cowboy.

The neckerchief of the open range cowboy kept the dust and dirt from getting down his neck; it could be pulled up over his nose to screen out the dust from a trail herd or a branding corral. It could also be used in

A "duded up" cowboy of the Judith Basin Pool and the open range. Note hat, neckerchief, fringed gloves, jacket, chaps and cowboy boots.

the late fall and early spring to keep his ears and face warm. In a strong wind the neckerchief could be used to tie his hat on his head. In a pinch it might serve as a dish towel or wash rag. It made a fair pigging string (a small rope carried in the pocket of every cowboy) when tying down a roped calf; it could be used as a throat latch or a head stall on a bridle. It might even enable the cowboy to hold the hot handle of a skillet. If he was lucky enough to have an extra kerchief, the cowboy could make it into a knapsack for small objects. The neckerchief was almost always bright red and made a handsome addition to the well-dressed cowboy's regalia when worn backwards or folded, but most of all it shielded his neck and face from the sun and wind.

Chaps, too, whether leather or angora, were an essential part of every open range cowboy's outfit. They provided him protection against cold, rope burns, cactus, thorn bushes, barbed wire, horse's teeth, cow or steer horns, and pouring rains, and if he were bucked off, the chaps might save him from serious injury.

The spurs that the early-day cowboys wore did jingle and attract attention, but they were also working tools. They helped him move his horse ahead to cross a deep or wide ditch or coulee, or urge his horse ahead when it was slow to move up on a calf, cow, or steer that was being roped or turned. Spurs helped a cowboy stay on a bucking horse or move an obstinate one into a needed position. Spurs moved a horse into action whenever and wherever the rider needed to go.

The high-heeled boots of the early cowboy had pointed toes to help him slip his foot into or pick up a loose stirrup. The heels kept his foot from going through the stirrup and prevented a rider from being dragged by a horse whether it was bucking, stumbling, or merely moving ahead. Boots gave the cowboy a comfortable hold on the stirrups as he braced against a roped cow, calf, or steer and allowed him to handle his rope much better. There is nothing on a boot to catch on a saddle or its stirrup. The high tops guarded against rope burns, barbed wire, and snakes. Like the chaps, the boots were also a protection from the teeth of a vicious horse or the horns of an angry steer. Boots worn in those open range days may have been decorated with a simple design, but mainly they were designed to keep the cowboy's feet comfortable and warm.

Cowboys often made their own rope of braided rawhide,[2] fifty feet in length and seven-sixteenths of an inch in diameter. It was made from a selected section of a two- or three-year-old beef hide that had been soaked in a solution of wood ashes and water for several days. After this, four very long strips of a one-half inch width were cut from it, soaked again, stretched with equal tension, and put out to dry. When the strips were completely dry, the hair was scraped off with a sharp knife and the strands were trimmed to a uniform width and length. The four strands were then rolled and soaked again for a day or two and once more trimmed and stretched. The finished strand was usually three-eighths of an inch wide and one-sixteenth of an inch thick. The four strands were then moistened for flexibility and braided into a single round rope. The rope was soaked again, trimmed with a sharp knife, and sandpapered for smoothness. It was then greased with beef suet and made flexible by pulling it through holes in a post or log, or by pulling it around a log. A honda, or eye, was then made in the loop end, and the strands on the other end were fastened so they would not unbraid. This rope was the cowboy's standby and was very durable, though very wet weather made it stiffen and often become unusable.

Trail-driving Texas cowboys used the Old Plains saddle with large Mexican horns, straight forks, half-covered seats, rolled cantles, large skirts, and double-rigging cinches. The Oregon men coming east to Montana used saddles that had full-covered seats, tall slender horns, small round skirts, center-fire rigging, or single cinches, and smooth bulges. Many riders using the Plains saddle simply threw away the rear cinch and some changed the rigging on the saddle to be like a single cinch. After 1879 most single rigs (cinch) saddles came with the men driving trail herds from Oregon.

There was little designing except for some on the flaps and skirt of the saddle. Some cowboys used the "Moran" with a discarded rear cinch and others the single-cinched "Oregon saddle." Another was the "Three-Quarter Rigged Montana" saddle.

Most stirrups were open and made of hardwood with laced leather around the base. Tapaderos, or stirrup covers, were not popular, and iron stirrups were too dangerous to use.

All saddles had a place for a rope on the right bulge (the front side of the saddle) and the ever-necessary saddle strings for tying on a slicker or a coat. Sudden hard rains were common in Montana, so most cowboys kept a slicker tied on back. There was an old saying, "The wise man takes his slicker when the sun is shining; any damn fool knows enough to take one when it's raining." And there was a line in one of the popular cowboy songs, "It's cloudy in the West and looks like rain and the darned old slicker's in the wagon again." Amby Cheney when reminiscing said "The cowboy's two biggest problems were how to winter a slicker and summer a girl."

Saddle blankets were folded once over. Some were plain, others were fancy in color and design. They were handmade or factory made. When off the horse, they could be rolled into a pillow or used for a ground cover or top blanket.

Bridles were leather with simple bits. Some cowboys used hackamore bridles. Once in a while a Montana cowboy would get ahold of a Mexican saddle and bridle loaded with silver trim to go with the hand-woven blanket. Charlie Russell told about one fellow who had a fancy outfit like that. They called him "Pretty Shadow" because he had no mirror (few cowboys did) so he was always watching his pretty shadow. They forgave him this bit of vanity because he was a top-hand—one of those cowboys who seemed to know what an old cow was going to do before she did it.

Every open range cowboy had a favorite horse, named him, and used him for special types of work. Kid Amby had "Old Gene," Timberline had "Big Roan," Teddy Blue Abbott had "Old Blue," Jack Emerson had "79," Al Malison had "Antelope," and Lee had the "Blue Mare."

Some horses were named because of their color, others for a brand they carried (79 or JB or Seven Up). Some were named for a friend or relative—like "Old Gene," "Billy," or "Black Bess." Other names that Amby remembered from his range-riding days were descriptive— "Cayuse," "Bones," "Wobbly," and "Dynamite."

When these early-day cowboys went out to ride circle, they used special horses from their string. If the assignment was to cut cows and calves into bunches for branding, a well-trained cutting horse was used. If they

Cavy of horses in a rope corral. These temporary corrals were constructed at each roundup camp site. The horse herder rounded the horses up each morning and put them in the corral so the cowboys could choose and catch the ones to ride for that day.
Photo courtesy of John B. Riggs of the Range Riders Museum of Miles City, Montana.

were to rope calves for branding, most men had a special horse for that job, too. If they were roping big six- or seven-year-old steers in the breaks of the Missouri or roping herd quitters, they needed a very strong rope horse. Working a trail herd required a strong, dependable horse, while nightherding a spooky bunch of steers took a calm horse that was very sure-footed and fast.

A few horses could be used for almost any purpose, but with a string of seven or eight horses a cowhand could, and often did, use three different horses in one day—one for early morning riding circle, one to work while helping with the branding, and another for nightherding.

Everything the open range cowboy wore, owned, used, or did had value to him in getting his job done in top-notch fashion.

Horse thieves were the most feared enemy of the open range men. Losing a valuable horse could put a man afoot so he couldn't do his work, get a job, or go anywhere. Horseback was the cowboy's only mode of transportation. Without a good horse, he simply could not operate. And besides, losing one's horse was like losing a good friend. Horse thieves were the most hated men on the range, and it is not surprising that, when they were caught, they were hanged immediately. This close relationship of a cowboy to his horse is shown in a line from a poem: "Tell me if you can, why the outside of a horse fits the inside of a man."[3]

Modern-day cowboys who spend their lives working with cattle on large ranches in the sagebrush country of the western states come nearest to matching the open range men. One can see them coming into town on

The same kind of gear—boots, hat, neckerchief, six-gun, and leather chaps—serve modern-day cowhands. Charles and Roy Cheney at a cow camp in the Little Belt Mountains.

Saturday night all slicked up in a clean shirt, Levis, boots, a Stetson hat, and a colorful neckerchief.

Many other people pay homage to the cowboy by imitating his dress. The image appeals to old and young alike.

Those open range cowboys are a part of history that passed with the building of fences and loss of unlimited ranges, but they have a place in our history along with the prospectors, the mountain men, the miners, and the covered wagon pioneers. Starting in the Southwest in the late 1870s, these cowboys had gradually moved their herds through the Midwest to Montana, Wyoming, and even into Canada.

By 1900, the days of the open range and big cattle pools were largely past in Montana, but the mystique and the romance of a cowboy on his horse lives on in our songs, our paintings, our rodeos, and in the dress-up western clothes we like to wear.

Cowboy and bronc rider, Fred Reed of Stanford, about 1928.

References:
[1] Vernam, Glenn, *The Rawhide Years* (Doubleday and Co., Garden City, NY, 1976). Reprinted "Enduring Mystique of the Cowboy," *Western Airlines* magazine, pp. 30-50.

[2] Oral explanations by Ambrose Cheney.

[3] Merica, Tim, "Tell Me if You Can." Framed, illustrated poem, c. 1984.

THE JUDITH BASIN CATTLE POOL
CHAPTER THREE

As the smaller ranges in southwestern Montana became crowded, the cattle owners began to look around for new pastures for their increasing herds. Granville Stuart[1] took a team and buckboard in early 1881 and went to look over the Judith Basin and areas to the south and east. He returned to Deer Lodge and reported enthusiastically that he had found a vast, well-watered pastureland where grass grew as high as saddle stirrups. He chose the Judith Basin because it had wonderful grass and was completely surrounded by mountains—the Little Belts were on the west and south, the Snowies on the southwest by the narrow Judith Gap, the Moccasins and the Judith Mountains on the east, and the Highwoods to the north.

The movement of cattle into the Judith Basin had actually begun in 1878 when T. C. Powers of Fort Benton and J. H. McNight of Fort Shaw brought their herds and joined H. P. Brooks, a pioneer in the Basin. They then formed the Judith Cattle Company which became the Judith Basin Cattle Pool soon after the southwestern cattlemen and local ranchers joined the organization.

Shortly after Stuart's return to Deer Lodge, the southwestern Montana cattle owners had decided to move their cattle to the new rangeland in the Judith Basin. Stuart and his partners, Davis and Hauser, then located their cattle company in the Judith area, but Fort Maginnis soon took over some of their chosen range, so the D.H.S. owners decided to graze their cattle on the northeast part of the Basin near the mining town of Maiden. Other cattle owners like Kohrs and Bielenberg, Kaufman and Stadler, Curtis and Pruitt, the Belcher Brothers, as well as Davis, Hauser, and Stuart, were all prosperous businessmen in Butte, Deer Lodge, or Helena. Each of them had several thousand head of cattle, which were sent to the Judith Basin with hired trail bosses and cowboys. Cattlemen like S. S. Hobson, Ensign Sweet, Frank Moury, Alex Tuttle, and Perry Westfall settled there with their own herds. Alex Tuttle was the first captain (or boss) of the newly formed Judith Basin Cattle Pool.

Judith Basin Pool cowboys on Rattlesnake Butte, northwest of Stanford. Amby and Melve Cheney second and third from the right.

Cowboys of the Basin Pool ready to ride circles. Far left—Amby Cheney; sixth from left, Melve Cheney; ninth from left, Gerard Berges.

Charlie Russell here is all "duded up." The cowboys knew him as a young man like this. He said he would rather be a poor cowboy (he was) than a poor artist which he certainly was not. *Photo courtesy of June Elklund Higgins and Patricia Morris*

The cowboys who worked the open ranges for the Judith Basin Pool drifted in from many areas. A number of them came with the trail herds. Young men in their teens like Amby Cheney and Charlie Russell came from the Midwest determined to be a part of the excitement of the new frontier.

At its greatest strength in the late 1880s, the cowboys of the Judith Basin Pool worked over 70,000 head of cattle (calves were never included in the count) on that grass-filled open range.

The cowboys who rode for the Judith Basin Pool and its successor, the Bearpaw Pool, often worked with Charlie Russell. Many of the tales they told centered around him, for he was a popular story-teller as well as an artist. He drew actual pictures of these roundups, and in his famous paintings, there are many portraits of his cowboy friends and sometimes their horses. This artist's skill in portraying real events and individual cowboys was demonstrated years later when two old cowboys went to view his painting, "The Roundup Leaving Utica in 1882." It had hung for many years on the wall of the old Mint Saloon in Great Falls. Although almost forty years had elapsed since then, Henry Keeton and Kid Amby Cheney were able to identify every man in the picture and even agreed on the names of the horses. Charlie always had a job as night-herder or horse-wrangler because he was such a good entertainer with his sketching and his stories.

Russell's artistry, even in his early days, was not in his painting alone. He always carried a lump of clay, and as one cowboy said, "We'd be riding along the trail and Charlie would pull a lump of clay out of his pocket. Without even looking at it, he'd work the clay with his fingers and when he finished, there would be a fine replica of whatever had caught his fancy at the time."

No other artist has preserved as much of the history of the big cattle pools as did Russell. In a painting of the roundup and branding of Judith Basin Pool cattle, he shows the hierarchy of the workers in the cattle business. According to Kid Amby, the bosses and the owners did the branding; the ropers (top-hands of the entire outfit) had to catch the calves by both hind legs, pull them over to the branders, and call out the brand to be put on each calf. The heelers and flankers then took over and held the calf for branding. If the calf got up and followed a cow with a different brand, the roper who had made the mistake was sent to the lowest job— that of holding the big bunch of cows and calves. Next highest in rank to the ropers were the cutters, who cut cows and calves out of the main bunch and put them in small groups with the same brand.

Usually the big group of cows and calves were held by the new hands, older men, or less able cowhands. Spring branding might go on for several days, and after that the crew might move to another herd on a different part of the range and continue with spring roundups and branding.

Kid Amby later recalled that Charlie Russell was a part of many of these roundups, but he was seldom sent to ride circle (gathering cattle from a designated area) because he was apt to find something he wanted to paint and stop right there. He'd throw the reins around the horse's neck, put his left leg around the saddle horn to make a sort of table, then reach in his back pocket for a piece of paper and stub of a pencil and start sketching. If he thought the sketch looked promising, he'd get a little metal box of water colors out of his back pocket, spit on the paints, and with a little effort, paint the picture. If he wasn't satisfied with a sketch or painting, he would just toss it away.

Roundup headquarters were established at Utica. The old T. C. Powers Trading Post there handled supplies that came up the Missouri River by boat. These supplies for cowboys and ranchers were brought into Utica by jerk-line teams and freight wagons from Clagett and Fort Benton. After 1880, the freight wagons picked up their loads at railroad terminals in Armington, Great Falls, and Lewistown. The stone building in Utica that

Cowboys of the Judith Basin Pool roundup about 1887. C. M. Russell is seated in the front row, third from the left. Amby Cheney and Henry Keeton could name them all and even knew their favorite horse. Other cowboys: Joe King, Johnny Sellers, Gene and Henry Gray, L. B. Taylor, Bert Jackson, Henry Kaufman, Jack Flynn (cook), Tom Waddell, Alec Tuttle, Jack Murphy, Zack Whitcomb, Pres. Larcum, Jesse Phelps, Henry Gates, Jean Martin, Terry McDonnel, and Charley Mattson. *Photo courtesy of Montana Historical Society, Helena.*

housed the Powers store is still in use as a post office and general store. Remnants of corrals built in the early days to hold cattle waiting for branding or shipping are still visible. A museum there now preserves many reminders of the past glory of Utica. Remains of those holding corrals can also be seen on Sour Dough Bench near Geyser and on the Louse Creek Bench east of Stanford.

After the fall roundups and brandings were over and the cattle were shipped to market, the horses and the remaining cattle were turned out to winter by themselves on the open range. Some of the cowboys were kept on for winter work with the cattle, some went home, and others just "holed up" in a cabin waiting for spring.

The cowboy's first spring job was to round up his own working string of horses. Usually in the latter part of May, when there was enough green grass to feed their horses, the cowboys came to Utica. Each one brought his string of horses—often as many as seven or ten because each cowboy had to furnish his own horses. Kid Amby said that at one time the men in the Basin Pool had 400 horses with forty different brands.

Noon camp of the Circle Diamond roundup, c. 1900. *Photo courtesy of Montana Historical Society*

Utica was a lively place for those few days. The headquarters of the outfits were set up on the flat below town, a few miles above Philbrook. From this base, the forty or more cowboys took their last fling at "civilization" before leaving town for the summer's work. Gambling was wide open, and the saloons were well-stocked with whiskey. Some cowboys had horse races on the Main (and only) street while their pals stood by and made bets as to who would be the winner. The store did a thriving business as cowboys bought a supply of blankets, clothing, and Star or Climax chewing tobacco. This was important because many of the roundup bosses and cattlemen argued that chewing tobacco wouldn't start prairie fires as the ashes from a cigarette or pipe might do. Cigarettes were unknown in Montana until the Texas and Mexican cowboys introduced them.

There was fun in Utica, but there was also work to be done. It was the busy season for bartenders, who relieved the thirst of cowboys and kept an eye on the gambling tables. Clerks were busy in the store selling soogans (quilts) and blankets for the cowboys' bed-rolls. But the summer wardrobe sales were meager because, at $40 a month, the cowboy couldn't afford much except a fairly good Stetson hat and a pair of leather boots. After those two important items, most anything would do—a suit of underwear, a pair of pants, and a shirt of blue chambray or black sateen. Of course he had to have a red kerchief and a good rope. If he hadn't been able to "winter" his yellow slicker, he'd have to buy a new one to tie on the back of his saddle.

Con Price, one of those old-time cowboys, reflected that "after a hard day's work, a fellow could unroll his bed and sleep soundly on the ground even if there were a few rocks under him." The only thing that frustrated him was getting his soogans spread out the wrong way so his feet stuck out and got cold before morning. Some of the soogans were almost square and the cowboys called them "sheepherders' quilts," explaining that was why the sheepherders went crazy, trying to figure out which way to put the quilt.

The owners in a cattle pool chose a roundup boss to organize the work of the three or four outfits that made up the pool. It required a man who was thoroughly knowledgeable about all phases of the cattle industry, who could work with the owners, and who could manage a crew of cowboys and a cook. The roundup boss was the liaison between the owners and the crew. With them he set up dates and places for branding, decided when, where, and what they would ship, and set dates for the spring and fall roundups. The boss was responsible for hiring, and if necessary firing, cowboys and deciding which ones would be kept on for winter work. Each day the boss assigned men to ride the different circles, and when the herd was being moved, he appointed the cowboys to the different positions—pointers in the lead, thinners (or swingers) along the sides, and the drags keeping the tail-enders going. The latter was the least favored position because of the dust stirred up by hundreds of moving

Cowboys of the Judith Basin Pool: left, Al Malison on Antelope (his rope is on the cow); Kid Amby Cheney in background on Old Gene; George Barrows (later the roundup boss); Frank Emerson on his horse "76"; and behind him Claude Dowen.

cattle. The boss assigned night-herders and the horse-wranglers, and he said who would drive the bed-wagon and the cook-wagon. He hired the cook and hopefully kept him appeased throughout a roundup season.

If it was Saturday night and the camp was anywhere near a town or a country school house dance, the boss decided who had to stay in camp and watch the herd while the others danced.

Plunkett was the roundup boss for the Judith Basin Pool during a period when it had over 60,000 head of cattle with three or four wagons (outfits) and 400 cow horses with forty different brands. Only Plunkett and Kid Amby knew all forty brands and who owned them. "Plunkett was a nice fellow and a good foreman when sober," said Amby, "but his drinking finally cost him his job."

Three cattle outfits were camped near Raynesford in old Cascade County. Two of the outfits belonged to the Judith Basin Pool and the third one was from the Shonkin Pool. The cowboys all went to the bar in Raynesford and most of them ended up drunk. Plunkett got in a fight with a cowboy named Dickson. The cowboys chose up sides and joined in the fray which lasted several hours. The only thing left undamaged in the saloon was the solid oak bar. Plunkett, who lost the fight, got Amby to take him back to the roundup camp. The cattle owners felt they had to replace him as top man of the Judith Basin Pool.

The camp cook was an important member of every outfit; he had to spend several days in Utica before each roundup laying in supplies. There had to be enough staples to last the season. He needed flour, dried apples and prunes, dry beans, coffee, salt, pepper, sugar, and a lot of sow-belly or salt pork and regular bacon—maybe a ham or two. That would be supplemented by fresh beef from the range. Cooking equipment and a stock of tin plates and cups remained in the cook's covered domain called the cook-wagon (or grub-wagon).

A good cook could serve three meals a day to a crew of forty wranglers. Occasionally he had to serve up a meal to the "coffee coolers," too. They were the cattle owners who came by to see that the roundup got off to a good start and kept going that way.

Every outfit had a bed-wagon that carried the canvas tarps in which each man had rolled his bedding and the few clothes that weren't on his back.

After a month or so on the range when a cowboy figured that his clothes should be washed, he could either take them and a bar of soap to a stream and slosh them up and down or take them over to the Widow Oats who lived along the Judith River. Her husband had died, and she was supporting herself and three daughters by doing washing for the cowboys. Sometimes she was called the "Swamp Widow" because of the kind of land she owned there. In later years, one of her grandsons, Bill Gallagher, who was an outstanding educator in Nevada, said he remembered his mother saying that "Grandma charged Charlie Russell three times as much as other cowboys because his clothes were three times as dirty." After Charlie met

This bedwagon and chuckwagon, belonging to the Spear O Cattle Company, are shown ready to move on to the next camp. *Photo courtesy of Elsa Speare Byron Johnson, Sheridan, Wyo.*

and married Nancy, he got "duded" up as fancy as any cowboy and wore the "breed sash" that became a trademark for him.

Each cowboy was expected to rope his own horse, saddle it, and be off to his assigned area by sunup. Russell wasn't too good with a rope then and Amby often roped his horse for him. Many years afterward, Russell came through Stanford on the way to his home in Great Falls and stopped to visit with his old friend, Kid Amby, saying, "Come here, I want to show you something I just learned." He took the coiled rope from Amby's saddle and began to spin it and jump through the loop. That was after he had been in California, and his friend, Will Rogers, had taught him some fancy roping tricks.

The two old friends reminisced and laughed about the time when the outfit was camped on the dry bench east of Stanford, where wood was scarce. Amby had noticed an old log shack from which the winter winds had blown the roof. The cook always needed firewood, so he hastily threw his rope over the top log of the cabin, planning to drag it back to camp. Almost before the log crashed to the ground, there was a loud yell, "Whatcha trying to do, Kid—kill me!" And there went Russell, running like a scared rabbit and holding up his pants with one hand. After a long shift of night-herding, he was trying to take a short nap before supper and was sleeping in the shade of the cabin. That big log that almost hit him could have cheated the West out of its most famous cowboy artist.

Happy was the roundup that had a good cook. After he had gathered some wood (or talked a cowboy into doing it), he'd have a good meal ready when the boys got in from riding circle. The dinner menu was often a repeat of breakfast and based on the staple fare of beef and beans. If he had time to prepare it, the cook might make a dried apple pie, or as a special treat, a "son-of-a-gun in a sack." This was a suet pudding with raisins or even one with a biscuit crust rolled out and filled with thick, syrupy candied tomatoes or any available fruit. Then the whole thing was rolled into a ball and wrapped in a piece of flour sack cloth and cooked in a kettle of boiling water. Fresh fruit was unheard of, so dried apples were a staple. There was an old cowboy saying, "It's a hell of a country where they call dried apples 'fruit'."

Every day in the roundup season began with the cowboys catching and saddling their horses. If anyone had chosen a horse that hadn't been ridden for some time, he might have to "top him off," riding around the camp until the horse quit bucking. Cold mornings put most horses in a bucking mood. Each man was assigned a circle by the roundup boss and was expected to round up all cows and calves in that area and bring them to the noon camp where they would be branded after dinner.

The cowboy's day began at sunrise, but long before that, the cook was up and had bacon, fried potatoes, sometimes beef-steak, and sourdough biscuits ready to be washed down with black coffee "strong enough to float an egg." He would beat on a tin pan with a big spoon and yell "Come and get it" to rouse the sleeping cowboys. By then the horse wrangler was in with the horses and had put them in a rope corral to hold them until after breakfast. The cowboys said they worked an eight-hour day—eight hours riding circle before dinner at noon and eight hours after dinner at the branding corrals.

After the noon meal, the real action started; different horses were saddled up for the branding job. Once again, there was apt to be an impromptu bucking contest. The branders built a roaring fire and put the irons in to heat. The cattle herd was brought in, and expert cutters sorted them into small bunches according to the cow's brand. A well-trained and intelligent cutting horse was necessary for this work. Next came the expert ropers, who began lassoing the animals to be branded. The bawling calves, which had to be caught by both hind legs, were pulled in close to the fire, and the roper called out the brand that was to be used. In the next instant someone flanked and threw the calf; a cowboy then put his feet against one front leg and on the neck while another worker grabbed one hind leg and put his foot against the other hind leg. They held it while the proper brand was being applied.

Some of the brands used by cattle owners in the Judith Basin Pool were Tuttle's upside-down hat on the left hip and Phelps and Pruitt's OH on the left ribs. Stadler and Kaufman used a bar under the tail and an R on the right ribs. Westfall used a W on the left shoulder. Winegard's calves were identified with a W Bar Dot on the left ribs; Hamilton had a flying O on the right ribs; Belcher used a dipper on the left ribs; Curtis put an F on both ribs; George Barrows branded with an O on the right hip and Phillips with a P on the right hip; and Ensign Sweet branded with Bar S the right ribs. (See illustrations of brands on pages viii-ix.)

At branding time, many of the owners in the various pools used ear, throat, or other additional markings such as a dewlap where the loose skin on the calf's lower throat was cut so it would almost drag in the grass, or the wattle which was cut up on the loose skin of the calf's lower throat so it waved around and could easily be seen. Sometimes one or both ears were split or cropped. These extra identification marks were most valuable when long hair or a poor brand made identifying the brand, and hence the owner, more difficult. Some outfits also used dots and bars, often under the tail or on the jaw, to help in identification. Male calves were castrated.

With all that done, the frantic calf was released to join his bawling mother. If the calf got up and had a different brand from his mother, the roper was in trouble. If they matched up, the brander called out the brand to the tallier, who marked it down for the owner. The roper needed not only skill but a knowledge of cowboy lingo. "Apple Orchard A" belonged to a man named Orchard, who branded with an A. "Railroad of the left ribs "meant two bars in that position; "Bar R" was a bar under the tail with an R on the right hip; "Hat steer" meant a steer branded with a hat, ⌐⌐⌐ . The position on the animal gave the clue as to which of the Tuttle brothers owned the calf because they all used the hat brand. Each brother had it recorded for a different place on the animal.

If a stray or maverick showed up in the bunch, it was branded for the association or was claimed by the man who found it. An old cowboy song tells of one way to dispose of such an animal.

> Stray in the herd and the boss says "Kill it,
> And hide that beef in the bottom of a skillet."
> Come a hi yi yip yipee yea.

Workers on every roundup outfit were always hungry for maverick steak or any kind of steak.

Amby Cheney related this story: "One time when our outfit was working near the badlands, a cow fell into one of those 'Bottomless' holes. Her head was farthest down and only her tail and hind feet were showing. Five of us hooked our horses onto the cow's hind legs but no amount of pulling would get her loose. After trying everything we could think of, we gave up and decided to put her out of her misery by shooting her. Though we couldn't get a shot at any vital organs, we fired a couple of shots and things quieted down. Hungry for beefsteak after days of salt pork, beans, and bacon, we figured there was no use letting all that fresh meat go to waste, so we lowered one of the fellows down to cut off some fresh meat. He hadn't any more than got a big steak cut off when that cow started to bawl. We got one meal of fresh meat out of that accident but for months afterward at night, I could distinctly hear that poor old cow bawling."

After an eight-hour session of branding, the dusty cowboys were glad to wash up and gather around the grub wagon for a hearty meal. Most of them were young, and after eating were ready to sit around the campfire in the evening swapping yarns or listening to some harmonica music and singing the cowboy ballads, even the mournful ones. "Little Joe the Wrangler," "Bury Me Not on the Lone Prairie," and "Get Along Little Doggies" were favorites. Sometimes there was a fiddler in the bunch or Mexican Joe Contlon with his guitar. Russell could play the melody with a cigarette paper over a comb. Amby could play it on his harmonica.

After the evening "sing" everyone could crawl into his bed-roll—except the night-herder, who had to saddle up again and stand guard. In good weather, the cowboys slept under the open sky and one can imagine them humming the tune to this song:

> On my saddle, I pillow my head
> And gaze at the bright stars in the sky
> And wonder if ever a cowboy
> Could go to that sweet bye and bye.

On the rare occasions when the roundup camp was within ten or fifteen miles of a country school house and a dance was scheduled, the cowboys rode over to do some socializing with the ladies. They would get out their

Getting a haircut in the early cowboy days. *Photo courtesy of Elmer Kelton*

best "duds" and if one of the crew happened to be the beau of the schoolmarm, all the others would chip in to dress him up in the brightest shirt available, a silk bandana, and even a ring, if anyone had one. There were never enough girls and women to go around, so the cowboys took along a handkerchief that they could tie on one arm to indicate they were taking the ladies' part in the lively round dances and quadrilles.

> Ladies to the right; gents to the left,
> Alleman left, meet your partner with a
> Double elbow swing, and promenade
> To you know where, and I don't care.

Even in the old log school houses, with men in cowboy boots, there were the more sedate dances, too—the French minuet, waltz, schottische, and the Varsovien.

Cowboys often created their own excitement, and one time they caused the first "black out" in Montana. A bunch from a roundup camp rode into the nearest town and shot out most of the windows and lights along the street. After once experiencing this cowboy boisterousness, the residents blew out the lamps and pulled down the shades whenever word came that the cowboys were coming to town. After a few drinks, the cowboys were also known to ride through the door of a saloon, rope furniture, and drag it into the street. Charlie Russell preserved this kind of escapade in his painting, "In Without Knocking."

These open range men had a whole series of corny jokes that went from one camp to the other like the one about the cowboy who was riding along with his girlfriend, Bella, near the Missouri River. Her horse fell and threw her off. He rushed up to her and said, "Did it hurtcha, Bella?" and she said, "No, but it hurt my back."

On cool evenings, the cowboys sat in the cook tent or the bed tent with their backs against the canvas wall. Curly Robinson thought it was fun to go outside and butt them hard with his head. The men got tired of this game, so they got a round, wooden stool and put it against the wall. Curly butted that once with his head, came away from the tent, said nothing, and never tried that trick again.

A major sport of the cowboys was horse racing, first among the men in their own outfit and then between cowboys of different outfits and other pools. Then, finally, they raced their best horses against the best horses of the Indians. They had bets, largely of money, between the cowboys, and then together they would take the best racing horse and put him up against the best Indian horse, betting money against blankets and buffalo robes. They didn't always win, because the Indians, too, had races among themselves to select the fastest horse for racing the best horses of the cowboys.

After the spring roundup was over, fewer cowboys were needed because the thousands of cattle were left to fatten on the rich prairie grass. The cowboys who were kept on worked the strayed cattle back to the outfit's home range. The others got jobs on ranches, or just hung around town and spent their wages while waiting for the fall roundup and another riding job.

The fall roundups were tougher than the spring ones. The days were cold and the beef cattle that were gathered in the fall had to be night-herded in snow storms and below-zero temperatures until it was time to ship them to market in Chicago or St. Paul. Cowboys had to exchange their slickers for coonskin or sheep-lined canvas coats and take an extra red bandana to tie around their Stetsons in place of a cap. Good wool or leather gloves were a necessity, and if a rider didn't have overshoes, he could wrap his feet in gunny sacks.

In these fall roundups the cowboys gathered all the three- and four-year-olds that had hidden out in past years. They also rounded up the dry cows and brought them with the steers back to camp and took turns herding them. Every cowboy took a two-hour shift at night. It was a pleasant task when it was warm and the skies were clear, but a rough one on a stormy night when the cattle would not "bed down." On those nights, the cattle milled around restlessly, frightened by the storm. Those were the nights when the cowboys sang to the herd or played their harmonicas. There seemed to be something soothing in the sound of a human voice and music that would quiet the animals and prevent a stampede. Singing or music also kept the other guard informed of where his partner was located.

Off to market with the cattle.

The town of Ubet was founded by A. R. Barrows and his wife, Augusta. Barrows ran a popular boarding house and was the first postmaster. Their sons, George and John, were top hands as cowboys. Ubet, Philbrook, Utica, Reedsport (Lewistown), Raynesford, and Old Stanford were some of the towns which were important to the Judith Basin Cattle Pool. *Photo courtesy of Meagher County Historical Society*

When driving a herd to a roundup for branding, to market, or even to a river crossing, two men worked as "pointers" to keep the cattle headed in the right direction. Then four "thinners" or "front and back swingers" rode on the sides and kept the animals stringing along, so they wouldn't bunch up or spread out too far. Two less-capable cowboys on the tail end of the herd had the "drags"—the old cows, young calves, and crippled animals—to contend with.

By the 1880s and 90s, practically all of the longhorns were natives. They had been raised in Montana.

At first the beef from the Judith Basin Pool had to be driven and grazed well over 100 miles to Billings to be loaded on the stock cars. Later, when the Great Northern was built into central Montana, the cattle could be loaded at Fort Benton. By the early 1890s, the Bearpaw Pool and other northern pools shipped cattle out of Malta and even later from Havre, which was then known as "Bull Hook Bottoms."

When the cattle were safely loaded on the railroad cars and on their way to market, accompanied by either the owners or a few cowboys, the fall work was over and the roundup crew disbanded. Again some of the cowboys went home, a few were employed as line riders or "reps" for the cattle companies, and some worked on the scattered ranches in the area.

A story is told about "Two Dot" Wilson,[2] who took several of his cowboys to help with the stock on a trip to the Chicago market. "Two Dot" got his nickname because his cattle brand was two dots—one on the shoulder and one on the thigh, which made it very difficult for a thief to alter. Two Dot, Montana, was named for this cattleman and his brand. He was never one for dressing up and, on this occasion, having arrived in Chicago with a load of cattle, he was arrested for vagrancy because he was so dirty and unkempt. He asked the policeman to accompany him to the bank, and when it was verified that Wilson had just deposited more than $10,000, he was set free. The incident had started as a practical joke; the cowhands who had accompanied Wilson to Chicago thought it would be fun to play a trick on the boss. They pointed him out to the police as a vagrant. But "Two Dot" found out about their conspiracy and went them one better. He took the next train home and left the cowboys in Chicago with neither money nor a return ticket.

But "back on the ranch" when winter set in, the cattle were left to shift for themselves, finding food on the windswept plains and shelter in the Missouri breaks or in brush along the streams. Most of them made it through if the winter was mild, but in tough winters like 1881-2 and 1886-7, thousands of them died. Again, Russell told the story with a sketch, this one of a lone, bony old cow, and he titled it "Last of the Five Thousand." It was a message to the cattle owners in response to their question about how the cattle had wintered.

Most of the cowboys "holed up" in a log cabin or a line-camp and batched until spring. They went out occasionally to "ride the grub line," visiting ranches in the sparsely settled country where western hospitality always made them welcome.

Because of the tremendous losses in those hard winters, and because of the increase of sheepmen and settlers, who were barb-wire (called "bob-wire") fencing their land, the cattle owners in the Judith Basin Pool began to look for more open ranges and greener pastures. In early 1890, some of them decided to move their cattle across the Missouri River to the Bearpaw Mountains and the prairies along the Milk River. Much Indian land had been opened up there, and the "Highline" railroad of the Great Northern had recently been built.

Just before the Judith Basin Pool cowboys started moving cattle across the Missouri River to the Bearpaws, they had one of the spring roundups and branding at the King Ranch near Lewistown. They brought in some 2,200 cows and their calves. All day long, the cowboys filled the larger corrals with cows and calves from their circles. Then the riders cut out half of the calves from the cows and put them in a smaller corral where the branding started. Kid Amby was one of those picked to be a roper because he used the backhand loop and could always pick up both hind legs of a calf. His friend, "Wild Bill" Sutter, another top roper, was also put to work. On that first day, they finished branding half the calves, and it took another day of roping, branding, and cutting before the other half of the calves could be turned out. The 2,200 cows and their freshly branded calves were then driven slowly toward the Missouri River crossing at Clagett. It was the first of many such herds to head toward the Milk River country and the Bearpaw Mountains. Some members of the Judith Basin Pool chose not to move their cattle to the Milk River country but established their own ranches in the Basin where they could keep their stock.

The men who brought the big herds of cattle into the Judith Basin worked as cowboys for awhile, but many of them eventually left the open range and took up ranches along the Judith River, Surprise Creek, Wolf Creek, or other streams. One of the towns in the Basin was later named for one of these men, S.S. Hobson, who had been an owner in the cattle pool. As early as 1881, James Fergus had already established a ranch on Arnell's Creek in the Judith Basin.

This big movement of herds out of the Basin and the turn to ranching marked the end of the Judith Basin Cattle Pool. The cattle owners who had moved their cattle to the Milk River country reorganized to form the Bearpaw Pool.

References:
[1] Stuart, Granville, *Journals and Reminiscences*, Vol. II (Arthur H. Clark and Co., Glendale, CA, 1957), pp. 94-144. (P. C. Phillips, Editor)

[2] Cheney, Roberta C., *Names on the Face of Montana* (Mountain Press Pub. Co., Missoula, MT, 1984), p. 272.

THE BEARPAW POOL
CHAPTER FOUR

The Bearpaw Cattle Pool was one of the largest organizations of cattle owners in those open range days of the late 1800s in Montana. It included the herds of some forty-five stockmen. It was formed when many of the Judith Basin Pool members joined other big outfits and pools and took their vast herds across the Missouri River into the Milk River country. There they joined with other owners already in the area and formed the Bearpaw Pool.

By 1890, the open range of the Judith Basin was about gone because of the influx of homesteaders and ranchers who had taken up most of the land around the water holes as well as the best pasture land. The decision of the cattle owners to move north called for a big roundup of range stock from the Judith Basin pastures during the summers of 1890 and '91. Great herds of cows, calves, and yearlings totaling over 150,000 from the D.H.S., the Moccasin, the Shonkin, the Judith Basin, and other cattle pools were eventually gathered and driven to Judith Landing. This spot where the Judith River flows into the Missouri was chosen for crossing the cattle because the river was shallow and more fordable at this point and the river banks were lower. It also gave easy access to the Milk River and Bearpaw mountain ranges with their greener and boundless pastures.

The cattle crossing made history at a spot already rich in history:[1] The Great Council of Indian Tribes was held there in 1854 and '55; Camp Cooke, the first military post in Montana Territory, was located there; the old PN Ferry carried hunters, trappers, and cowboys across the Missouri there, long before the river was bridged. Judith Landing (also called Clagett or Camp Cooke) was an early-day settlement just above Cow Island which was the head of navigation in the late dry summers when steamboats could not reach Fort Benton because of low water. The cargoes had to be unloaded and taken from there by jerk-line freight wagons overland to Fort Benton. From that town, the goods were distributed to the gold mining camps of Bannack, Virginia City, and Last Chance Gulch, and to the Whoop-up Trail toward Lethbridge and Medicine Hat in Canada.

The name of the settlement was changed from Camp Cooke to Clagett in 1872 when Billy Clagett, the camp cook, was elected to Congress. Five people had turned out to vote and hold an election.[2]

After years of being almost deserted, the little place came to life during the summer of 1890 and '91, when the cowboys moved thousands and thousands of cattle across the river there.

There were four outfits from the Judith Basin Pool, each one with eight or ten cowboys, a cook, a night-herder, and a horse-wrangler. The Moccasin, Shonkin, and other pools each had two, three, or four outfits working the crossing. Each outfit had rounded up between 2,000 and 3,000 head of their cows, calves, and yearlings, cutting back the dry cows and beef steers before heading the cattle toward the river. Night-herding of the cattle before the crossing was a big job because the animals were apt to break away and return to a previous bed ground. A loud shout would have frightened the cattle and caused trouble.

Every outfit from the pools made several trips back to the home range during the summer of 1890 to bring cattle to Judith Landing. On each trip the big problem was to keep cows and calves from turning around to head for their previous bed ground. Sometimes the drag-end cowboys had to rope a calf or two to force them to return to the moving herd.

The river was high from the June run-off and the cattle were afraid of the roaring water. The big job now for the cowboys was to head the animals into the Missouri and then get them across. Kid Amby said they used every trick they could think of to get them across the Missouri. One scheme was to head them into the sun, so they couldn't see too well, and after a few animals had gone in, others would follow. Another plan was to hold the cattle on the high bluffs for two days until they were so thirsty that the leaders rushed eagerly into the river and the whole herd followed, urged on by the yells and ropes of the cowboys. Sometimes the men used cottonwood logs to make a chute into the river and drove the cattle into it. If a cowboy roped a calf and took it across the river in the ferry boat or behind his horse, the mother cow would plunge in to follow her bawling offspring. Led by that cow, others would follow. The calves were smart enough to swim on the down-river side of their mothers. Horses were sometimes driven into the river and cattle pushed in behind them. When the cattle were swimming in the river, only their heads and horns could be seen above the surface.

If a cowboy got thrown or his horse fell during a crossing, he knew that his best chance of getting to land on the other side was to grab the tail of a horse or a cow. The men who worked these Missouri River crossings became so expert that they ended that gigantic job without loss of cowboy, cow, or horse. "A hundred-fifty-thousand head across that river, and we never lost a cow or cowboy," Kid Amby later recalled with pride as he told of those crossings in 1890 and '91.

The old PN Ferry was an important part of the big crossing, too, as the chuck-wagon, bosses, and bed-wagons of some twenty outfits and

Seven Bearpaw Pool cowboys relax by the grub wagon. At right are Melve and Amby Cheney.

Four cowboys of the Bearpaw Pool, left to right, Amby and Melve Cheney and two unidentified cowboys.

some of the cattle owners had to be ferried across the river.

In the summer of 1890, the cattle were crossed in bunches of 2,000 to 2,500 head, and it was a tough job for even the most seasoned cowboy as the mighty Missouri was a river to be reckoned with. The cowboys often fortified themselves with Bill Norris's whiskey which, according to legend, was strong enough to make the Missouri River look like Wolf Creek. The men and horses got so used to swimming and to being wet that it was a common occurrence for someone to call out, "Come on, guys, let's have a drink at Bill's" and every man who could leave the herd would jump on his horse, "split the Missouri wide open," and hurry to the saloon.

These crossings were continued by the Judith Basin Pool until sixty or seventy thousand head of cattle and thirty or more cowboys were safely settled in the areas east of Havre, south of the Canadian border, along the banks of the Milk River, and on the fringes of the Bearpaw Mountains. Westfall, Hamilton, Hobson, the Skeltons, and several other owners did not move their cattle, so it is safe to say that the Judith Basin Pool at its peak had seventy to eighty thousand head of cattle.

The summer of 1891 brought a small-scale repetition of the great crossing. L. B. Taylor had been chosen as boss of the newly organized Bearpaw Pool, and he and the other pool bosses sent cowboys back to the Judith country to gather any strays. Straggling herds of cattle were gathered by all the pools and outfits that still had some cattle in the eastern part of the Judith Basin. These smaller herds were taken across the Missouri to join the others in the Milk River country. Some of the cowboys had cut out the dry cows and steers. They drove those to Billings for shipment to Midwest markets. On those drives the men had to be careful not to let their animals mix with those of the "79" outfit as the Judith cattle were trailed through "79" range, near and around "Big Dry Coulee," some fifty miles northwest of Billings.

Plunkett had been the roundup boss while the big herds were being moved to and across the Missouri River, but he had a serious alcohol problem, and when the new pool was formed, the owners decided to replace him with Taylor, who had taken up a ranch in the Bearpaws. Taylor's ranch then became the headquarters for the new Bearpaw Cattle Pool. It was near Lloyd, a community made up of a saloon, store, and post office, located on Snake Creek in Blaine County. Lloyd got an official post office in 1890, and the Dolans ran the store. Mail and supplies had to be hauled by four-horse teams from Chinook. Kid Amby remembered opening a big Christmas box that he got through the Lloyd post office and finding only a few crumbs of what he assumed had once been a cake.

Many top hands who had worked the river crossing were hired on with the newly formed Bearpaw Pool. Among these transfers from the old Judith Basin Pool were Al Malison, Con Price, George Barrows, Horace and Charlie Brewster, Frank Spencer and his brothers, Charlie Russell, Amby Cheney and his brother, Melve, and their half-brother, Gerard Berges,

Cowboy funeral in Northeast Montana. Possibly the funeral of Al Mollison of the Bearpaw Pool. *Photo courtesy of Mrs. Pearl Coombs and Farr and Toole, Montana Historical Society, Helena.*

"Wild Bill" Sutter, Johnnie Crothers, Gus Hammer, Henry Keeton, Sid Willis, Joe Dickson, Pete Vann, Kid Curry, Charlie and Ad Carthrae, Frank Pruitt, and the Weaver Brothers, who had come in from the Oregon cattle country.

Over the years, the following men were some of those added to the list of Bearpaw Pool cowboys: Tom Ross, Johnny Brinkman, Slim Trumbel, Frank Ryan, Johnny Auld, Long George Francis, Johnny Lee, Al Rehberg, Baldy Buck, Pecos, Bill Masterson, Frank Barnum, Claude Dowen, John Griffin, Johnny Mathison, Curly Robinson, John Thompson, Kid Lowry, Tony Crawford, Jim Turnbull, Billy Rowe, Lawrence Gee, Charlie McGuire, Harry Green, Byron Connelly, Ed Rhodes, Joe Doles, Charlie Parks, and Bob and Charlie Stuart.

Bearpaw roundup bosses who followed Taylor were Horace Brewster, George Barrows, and Frank Pruitt. Barrows gave instructions to his men about handling a bronc: "Forefoot him, saddle him up, fork him, and then tie your bed-roll on him." Barrows once said that his three best cowboys were Kid Amby as a roper, and Con Price and Charlie McGuire as riders.

Every big pool chose reps to ride through other pools' herds to pick up any of their cattle that had gotten mixed in with the wrong bunch. This was especially important during the roundups for branding or shipping and while moving cattle to a new range. Repping for the Bearpaw Pool meant being present at all other pools' roundups, brandings, and shipments. The reps had to check for all the forty-five members' brands and turn back or move toward the home ranch any cattle belonging to any owners in the Bearpaw Pool. Repping also included checking all cattle being sold or driven out of the neighboring Circle C ranch's area to see if any Bearpaw Pool brands were in the bunch. Reps like Long Henry, Teddy Blue Abbott, Con Price, Humpy Jack Davis, and Kid Amby Cheney were among the highest paid, most dependable, and hardest working cowboys. They were kept on the payroll during the winter when most of the cowboys holed up or rode the grub line.

A carload of orphans once arrived in Chinook, and Jim Bone took a little humpbacked boy home to carry slop to his pigs. That little boy, Humpy Jack Davis, later became one of the best riders and reps in Montana.

If a cow outfit from another pool shipped Bearpaw Pool cattle, paying no attention to the rep, he could black-ball them and put them out of the Livestock Association and that would cause them all kinds of difficulty, legal and otherwise.

As each of the big outfits began to work its range, the men established a "day herd" of cattle made up of those the reps from other outfits had cut out and wanted held, usually to take to their home range or ranch. With no fences to mark range boundaries, it was very difficult to keep the herds from mixing. There were often six or seven reps from different outfits, so the day herd that was held on the bedground might number several thousand. This was often called a rep outfit. The reps never did any day-herding, and only on special occasions would one of them night-

A roundup camp. Cavy of horses in a rope corral, bed tents, and campwagons. *Photo courtesy of Range Riders Museum Miles City, Mont. and John B. Riggs.*

herd. He was busy enough checking for his outfit's branded cattle and bringing them into the day herd. Other cowboys from their home outfits usually herded these reclaimed animals. If a rep had too many cattle to move, he'd send word back to headquarters to get more cowboys to help.

Every outfit carried "running irons," which consisted of a small bar and small half-circle. With those, almost any brand could be made. The men would often brand a calf with its mother's brand as they found it on the range.

If animals had wandered too far from the home range and were shipped to market with another bunch, the money from the sale of those branded cattle was sent to Helena to be held for the rightful owner according to the Livestock Commission records.

Open range night-herders were assigned according to need; a herd of cows and calves gathered for branding might be easily handled by one or two men, while a beef herd with some renegades (or herd-quitters), big steers, or Texas longhorns from the trail might require a larger crew, which meant a changing of the guard every two or three hours.

To quote Amby Cheney, "Lightning and thunder could cause problems, but we were never sure just what caused a herd to stampede. If the cattle started to run, the best way to handle the situation was for one of us to get to the point or front of the herd and try to turn them in a circle with other men keeping those behind turning the same way. When we were on night guard, we tried to use our surest-footed and most dependable horse, and we'd always try to prevent a herd split. Sometimes on a very quiet night with sort of a spooky tenseness, a few sudden noises like the crashing of a tree could start a herd on the run. If one or two animals bawled, the run would usually stop, but if the herd split, we would have to run them back together and this meant some broken horns and crippled cattle." Stopping a stampede was a tough and dangerous job, and many a good cowboy was killed when his horse stumbled as he tried to stop or turn a frantic herd.

And they sang about it around the campfire on those summer evenings. In later years, Amby sang his children to sleep with ballads like "When the Work's All Done This Fall,"

> That very night the cowboy went out to stand his guard.
> The night was dark and cloudy and storming very hard.
> The cattle all got frightened and rushed in wild
>   stampede.
> The cowboy tried to turn them while riding at full
>   speed.
> His saddle horse did stumble and upon him did fall.
> The boy'll not see his mother when the work's all done
>   this fall.

The work of the Bearpaw Pool fall roundups went on much the same as it had in the Judith Basin Pool, winding up with shipping time when beef cattle were loaded on railroad cars at Chinook or Malta and sent to market in Chicago. Shipping time was always lively. Not only were the cowboys back in town after a long fall work session, but most of the owners also came to see their cattle loaded.

During one of the later years of the Bearpaw Pool, when the cattle herd was being held out on the flat near the stockyard, there was an old steer who had escaped shipment each year by hiding in the breaks and badlands along the Missouri. Every time the cowboys got this six-year-old near the loading chute, he managed to break away.

Finally, one exasperated cowboy spurred his horse, rode up close to the steer, and leaning over, grabbed his tail and deftly twisted it around the saddle horn. Instead of stopping the steer, so great was the momentum that the tail broke off and a stream of blood spurted over the cowboy and his horse. The owner of the steer was an old German, Abe Kaufman, from Helena. Abe was perched on a fence and began shouting, "Fire dot cowboy! Fire dot cowboy! He's too rough." The big steer, tamed by this experience and the loss of his tail, walked meekly into the loading chute. The cowboys who had witnessed the scene started laughing and shouting, "Fire dot cowboy, fire dot cowboy." Kid Amby didn't get fired. He had worked for the Bearpaw Pool for several years and was a top roper, circle rider, and rep to the Circle C and Square outfits.

Melvin Cheney on his horse. Judith Basin Pool cattle grazing at Sunset. *Photo courtesy of Chris E. Morris, Chinook, Montana. Picture printed in Germany. Used here with permission from Caralee Cheney. Photo from collection of Mrs. Melvin (Grace) Cheney.*

When the cattle train pulled out for Chicago, a number of the owners and cowboys rode in the caboose. Their job on the trip was to see that none of the cattle lay down in the railroad cars where they would be trampled to death. The men often took their own food, carefully packed in a shoebox. They saw to it that the cattle were fed and watered at the stockyards en route to Chicago, as the law required. Stops were often made at Minot, New Rockford, and St. Paul to feed the cattle.

The last whistle of the engine, as it puffed around the curve heading away from the Montana loading chutes, signaled the end of the fall roundup. The cowboys not on the train were free to scatter for the winter. As always, a few went home while some got jobs on the ranches or as line camp riders to see that the cattle did not stray from the home range.

Most of the Bearpaw Pool cowboys, however, holed up for the winter in some convenient cabin and batched until time for the spring roundup. One winter, a group known as the "Lousy Seven" holded up in an old cabin in Chinook. It didn't take long for them to get rid of their fall wages. Food was getting scarce at the cabin, and some of the housewives of the town were beginning to complain of chickens missing from their hen houses. Early in December, the cattle owners in Helena got word of the cowboys' plight. Good cowboys were hard to come by, and the owners couldn't afford to let this bunch starve to death, so they sent word to Al Malison, one of the Lousy Seven, that he could butcher a beef for them to eat.

Just a few days before Christmas, when the men were getting tired of a straight beef diet, Kid Amby rode into town. He had been employed at the headquarters for the winter because he knew all the brands of the horses in the herd. At that time, his job was to keep the horses from crossing the river and going back to their old home in the Judith Basin. When Amby arrived in town, he had his month's wages, a check for $40, in his pocket. He had planned to send it to his mother for Christmas, but he decided to go see his old pals before he went home. He wanted to visit with them, but he didn't plan to stay overnight as he knew they had body lice and those varmints were hard to get rid of. He found the Lousy Seven full of beef steak, but hankering for some whiskey for Christmas cheer. Before he knew it, Amby had "loaned" them his whole $40. They promised to pay it back the next spring out of their first wages, but by spring they would no doubt have forgotten all about it.

Among cowboys, a loan of less than $10 was never even considered for repayment. Amby never regretted making that $40 loan, but he was sorry he hadn't held Russell to his promise that he would paint him a picture of the Lousy Seven. As Amby recalled the group, they were Charlie Russell, Al Malison, Kid Lowry, George Barrows, John Thompson, Tony Crawford, and Jim Turnbull.

Amby never did get the promised painting, and soon after that, Russell was married and his wife, Nancy, began to market his pictures for "fabulous" prices to the Easterners who were coming in large numbers to the

"When Ropes Go Wrong" by C.M. Russell. Riders believed to be Circle C cowboys, Will, Bob, and Wallace Coburn. *Photo print used by courtesy of Bradford-Brinton Museum, Big Horn, Wyo.*

dude ranches that were just getting started in Montana. The dudes came to try to experience the rustic life of the cowboys that they had heard so much about. Some of the dudes were lucky enough to hear Charlie Russell spin his yarns about those early days in the West.

Amby missed another chance to have a Russell original. One day when he was riding through some brush along the Missouri River Badlands, he caught sight of a piece of paper fluttering from a wild rose bush. He swung his horse over that way, reached down and got the paper but found it was only one of Charlie's sketches of cowboys and horses. Amby speculated, "I might have made a thousand dollars if I'd kept that picture."

It was the spring after Amby's Christmas visit to the Lousy Seven that John Thompson, one of the group, spent too much time at the bar—as usual—with his fellow cowboys. As they went to the hitching rack to get their horses, planning to head straight for the Bearpaw Pool's roundup camp at the edge of Bull Hook Bottoms, John spotted a group of Indian teepees at the "half-breed encampment" near town. This encampment was known to be one of the toughest places in the country—cowboys, Indians, and Negro soldiers hung out there.

John decided on a little ornery fun and began roping the teepees and dragging them away. He wound up with his saddle under his horse, and he was where the saddle should have been. The half-breeds were cursing and throwing rocks and bottles. His friends were on their horses on the sidelines, laughing at John, but they managed to help him get his saddle

Cowboys of the Bearpaw Cattle Pool. Photo taken in Big Sandy 1895. Melvin Cheney, center top row. Amby Cheney, lower left. Upper right, friend of Grace Cheney, shown also in Chapter 3 as "duded up" cowboy. *Photo courtesy, Montana Historical Society.*

righted so they could all get back to the roundup camp for work.

Roping teepees seemed to be a favorite sport as another time Guy Tullock (later sheriff of Fergus County) decided that cowboys should have fun when they came to Bull Hook Bottoms so he roped a teepee, took a dally around his saddle horn, and spurred off. The breeds chased him for quite a while, throwing rocks and bottles but never hitting him.

Later in the summer after the teepee roping episode, the Lousy Seven lost one of their men. Lousy Al Malison was a gambling cowboy but a good worker and well-liked by his associates. He got on a Diamond S horse named Billy, but the horse threw him. As he went off, the horse kicked him in the leg and head. When the other cowboys reached Al, he was lying on the ground with a bone sticking out of his leg. They picked him up and took him to the hospital in Fort Benton, but he soon died of his injuries. His funeral was a sad one for his many cowboy friends. Kid Amby was one of the pallbearers.

Death and pain were no strangers to the cowboys of the cattle pools. Frank Barnum, one of the Bearpaw Pool cowboys, had a toothache, and after he did a lot of complaining about the pain, his friends got him to go to the dentist in Fort Benton. He wasn't sure he should take a chance on the dentist, so a number of the boys went along to give him courage. They watched from the street to see how things were going. All went well until the dentist started pumping his treadle machine, hit a tender spot in Frank's mouth, and made him jump. The machine got caught in Frank's whiskers and the cowboys got a good laugh as the dentist and patient tried to untangle the machine from Frank's beard.

Frank and his wife later settled at Lloyd and their good-looking daughter, much to the disappointment of the cowboys, married Indian Charlie.

Rattlesnakes were an ever-present danger for the cowboys. One hot summer day, when the roundup was camped out on Sun Prairie north of the Bearpaw Mountains, the men were sitting around in the shade of the tent after dinner. Charlie Russell, who had herded the horses all night, was lying on his back fast asleep and snoring. The tent flaps had been fastened up to let a cool breeze blow through the tent. The cook was gathering up the pie pans, which served as plates, and the tin cups, when suddenly he gasped, motioned for silence, and pointed to a huge rattler. The snake had entered the tent and was crawling slowly toward Russell. In breathless silence, the cowboys watched the snake as it crept toward their friend and slowly crawled across his belly, then slithered out of the tent on the other side. As soon as the snake left the tent, the men jumped up and put an end to it with their six-guns, sticks, and rocks.

Charlie was awakened by their shouts and the shots and, at first, didn't believe their story, but they had the dead snake for evidence and even the cook corroborated the story. Charlie didn't dare doubt the cook's word because a good cook was a most valuable asset and had to be treated with great respect. If a cook didn't like the way the cowboys treated him, he was apt to jerk off his flour-sack apron, climb on his horse, and head for town, leaving the men to do their own cooking until the owner could send out a new cook.

The cow camp menu was never fancy—lots of beans and bacon, hardtack or biscuits, and once in a while some canned fruit. Then there were prunes—a "Geyser dish" was three of them soaked and stewed and meted out. The term was left over from Judith Basin Pool days when they ranged cattle near the town of Geyser.

Sometimes there would be fresh beef or venison, but it didn't last long due to hearty appetites and hot weather during spring and summer. Thick slices of ham were a rare treat and were especially welcome in the lunches that the cook put up for the men who were riding a wide circle. In the cook tent, grub was occasionally set out for the men to eat between meals, and if the weather was really cold, they might be allowed to warm themselves by the cook's stove.

Horace Brewster, who was the roundup captain after Taylor, was scuffling with a friend one day, and they upset some of the bread that had been set to rise in large dripping pans. The cook, who was known as "Greasy Tom," pulled off his apron and threatened to quit. Brewster raised his wages $5 a month to get him to stay, so he then made $60 a month—the top wage in the crew. Cowboys were earning $40 a month plus food, and they furnished their own bed-rolls. Reps to other cattle pools got from $45 up because they were skilled men who knew all the home outfits' brands and could spot and retrieve the bosses' cattle that had mixed in with other herds.

After the Rustlers' War in Wyoming, the cattlemen there chased most of the "wanted dead or alive" men out of the state, and other cowboys just left because of the trouble. Many of these fugitives, good and bad, drifted to Montana. Cowboys were scarce and were usually hired with no questions asked. One of the so-called "rustlers," known only as Pecos, was taken on by the Bearpaw Pool. One morning he was ready to go on circle and no lunch was ready for him to take as the cook was grumpier than usual and slower, but was tossing some bacon toward the frying pan. The new cowboy, anxious to be on his way to ride circle, walked into the cook tent to put up his own lunch. He found some apple pies cooling and cut a piece for himself. That was something few cowboys would ever dare do as the cook tent was strictly out of bounds. When the cook saw Pecos take the pie, he was so angry he slapped the cowboy on the face, picked up a butcher knife, and chased him out of the tent. Whereupon the cattle-rustler-turned-cowboy went to his bed-roll, took out his gun, and shot the cook. Then he picked up his bed-roll, jumped on his horse, and took off. Not one of the cowboys tried to stop him as there was no need for another person to get shot.

Bill Masterson was dispatched to Chinook to notify Roy Clary, the Chouteau County sheriff at Fort Benton. But by the time the officer of the law traveled the long distance from the county seat, the trail was cold and Pecos had made his escape. Perhaps he went back to the Hole-in-the-Wall region in Wyoming, which was famous as an outlaw hide-out.

The cook was buried in the cemetery at Chinook. Even today in that long-neglected plot may be seen the headstone erected by the cattle owners over the grave. That was a century ago, but the name of the cook, Frank Mitchell, is still legible on the stone.

Before the Wyoming renegades came, the Montana cowboys had considered themselves well armed with one six-shooter. Then they had to adopt the fashion of the Wyoming "two-gun" men and carry a gun in each holster strapped to their sides. The Montanans had learned to draw cross-handed so the guns and holsters were turned backwards and used that way. The Wyoming cowboys had their guns forward and drew them straight from each side. There were arguments about the merits of the cross-handed or straight-handed draw, but exponents of each method competed and the straight-ahead draw proved the faster.

Wyoming cowboys continued to drift into Montana. Some came because of the trouble there, and they objected to the ruthless killing of homesteaders who were falsely accused of being rustlers. Others, like the Curry brothers, who were part of Butch Cassidy's gang, came because they were wanted for crimes in Wyoming. Many of the law-abiding men found work on northern Montana ranches or with the roundups and eventually settled on the land there.

Long Henry was one of the Wyoming cowboys who came to Montana. He became a rep for the Circle Diamond during the same time that Kid Amby repped for the Square or Millner outfit. The headquarters for the Square outfit were in the Little Rockies east of the Bearpaw Mountains and near the Circle C, owned by the Coburns. The Circle Diamond was the brand of the Bloom Cattle Company operating near Malta. Amby said that Jack Teal of the Circle Diamond was a husky fellow with beady eyes who was always wrestling with other cowboys and that Long Henry was no match for him in a rough and tumble battle but it didn't matter because that wasn't the way Henry operated. He had his eye on Tommie Dunne (Starr), who had signed on with the Circle Diamond, too. The men knew that Dunne was a man who had reasons for leaving Wyoming, but only Long Henry knew his real identity. Everyone had heard of the outlaw, Starr. There was no obvious quarrel in the camp that night, but when Starr bent over to picket his horse, Long Henry shot him. Both of them had been involved in horse stealing, but why the partnership ended this way, no one except Henry knew.

It wasn't only the Wyoming men who caused violence amongst the Montana cowboys; shooting scrapes were common when the cowboys were on a drinking spree in town. Johnny Brinkman once remarked that Charlie Russell had the knack of getting himself into more "jack-pots" than anyone else—like the time in Malta, when a crowd of cowboys were in a saloon and a drunken sheepherder came in. The herder had been robbed in a card game and was angry, so he began shooting up the place.

Bedlam reigned and the cowboys made a dash hoping to get out the back door. Next to the outside door, there was another door that led into a dusty, unused closet under the stairs. In the confusion, someone opened it by mistake and several of the men rushed in. When the herder was disarmed and the smoke cleared away, the fellows came back in through the two doors. They looked around for Russell but couldn't find him. There was a loud shout when the last man came out of the closet. It was Charlie covered with dust and cobwebs. He had been the first man to go in the wrong door and had been pushed by his followers clear back under the stairway.

Charlie lost out on another occasion, too. There was a dance in town and one of the guys was fixin' up to take his girl. Every cowhand in the camp helped by donating the best he had. Together they came up with new boots, a white silk shirt, red silk bandana, and a belt with a fancy buckle, so the lucky cowboy could make a good impression. As a finishing touch, Russell loaned him his new gold ring. Well, there was some kind of a shooting scrape at the dance that night and that poor cowboy got killed. The coroner shipped the body back east to his mother, and Russell's ring went right along and was buried with that cowboy. Russell felt badly about losing that ring.

Another romance that had a surprise ending was Gus Hammer's. Gus was one of the toughest guys in the Bearpaw Pool. He rode into town one night to see his girl. She persuaded him to go with her to a revival meeting that was being conducted in Chinook that night by a Methodist minister. So powerful was the sermon preached by the Reverend Martin that Gus got religion! He was a changed man! Gus was the only minister to come out of the Bearpaw Pool bunch.

Very few of the open range cowboys were really outlaws, but they all liked to whoop it up on their trips to town and sometimes got in trouble. Most of them had come from good homes in the Midwest or the East, and they were often a happy-go-lucky bunch who had been lured to the West by a desire for adventure. They found a lot of hard work along with the excitement of being a part of the big, open range cattle pools.

In addition to the Judith Basin and the Bearpaw Pools, there were many other pools and outfits in central and northern Montana during the open range period. One of the earliest was the Chestnut Valley Roundup with headquarters at Cascade. They ranged their cattle as far east as Belt Creek. John McGiffin was a long-time cowboy with this outfit; Abner McGiffin worked often in the spring and summer; and Nat McGiffin, later to be Kid Amby's father-in-law, worked with them for a short time.

The Shonkin Pool ranged from the Highwoods east to the Missouri and later across the river from Fort Benton to Big Sandy. It eventually became a very large outfit and moved across the border to Canada. Ad and Charlie Carthrae worked for this outfit.

The Circle C outfit belonged to Robert Coburn and his three sons—Bob, Will, and Wallace. Walt Coburn, the writer, was half-brother to them

"Real Westerns," North Montana Fair, Great Falls, August 22-26, 1932. Top: Pete Knight, Kid Amby, Johnny Brinkman, Billie Buck, Guy Wheatie. Bottom: Sid Willis, Powder River Jack, Harry Knight.

and just a toddler when they were running the ranch. The three older boys were said to have "notches in their guns," and at times were associated with the Currys, and for a short time with Butch Cassidy. The Coburns were located in the Landusky and Zortman country in the Little Rockies. In commenting about Walt Coburn's wild west stories, someone said that Walt had a good imagination. "Imagination, hell," said Kid Amby, "all he had to do was write about his brothers."

The D.H.S. outfit, owned by Davis, Hauser, and Stuart, has been described earlier. They were often called the Damned Hard Set by cowboys in other outfits.

Hank and Ed Shoefelt had the TL outfit. One time they bought a "never been ridden" horse from Canada. They bet that even Long Henry, who rode their rough string, wouldn't be able to ride him. Cowboys from the TL put up wager money from their poker earnings and lost it all because Long Henry rode that Canadian horse to a show-down. Kid Amby and Con Price both repped for the TL outfit for a while.

The H Cross, or Roberts Cattle Company, was owned by Zeke and Barry Roberts. The Long S outfit, belonging to Ed Fox, ranged along the Musselshell near the present town of Mosby. Charley Stuart and Fred Gibson worked for both of these outfits. The "7-77" outfit was part of the "79" spread and ranged cattle northwest of Coulson (now Billings).

The Bearpaw Pool was one of Montana's last big cattle pools, as these organizations depended on free access to the open ranges. When that land was settled, an era ended, and the open ranges of central and northern Montana became a land of homesteads and small ranches.

References:
[1] Cheney, Elizabeth McGiffin, "The Old PN Ferry," unpublished ms.

[2] Cheney, Roberta C., *Names on the Face of Montana* (Mountain Press Pub. Co., Missoula, MT, 1983), pp. 52-53.

[3] Interview with Ambrose Valencourt (Kid Amby) Cheney.

[4] Coburn, Walt, *Pioneer Cattleman in Montana, The Story of the Circle C Ranch* (Univ. of Okla. Press, Norman, OK, 1968), p. 15 & ff.

CATTLE AND HORSE THIEVES
CHAPTER FIVE

The problems of rustling, homesteading, and mave-ricking (the branding of unmarked cattle) were tapering off in Texas as many of the big outfits were moving north to the open ranges of Wyoming and Montana. In both states cattle and horse stealing soon developed into a major problem. Wyoming was first to take action in dealing with the rustlers. Their Stockgrower's Association had over "400 members and all but 80 of them owned over a thousand head of cattle." Initially they had plenty of free land and wonderful grass. They soon began to realize that cattle thieves, as well as bad weather and predators, were cutting into the profits. They made a frantic and ill-planned attempt to solve their problems by passing the "Maverick Bill" in 1884. It was so unfair that anybody named by the big outfits as a "rustler" was immediately out of the cattle business and in danger of being hanged. A common saying was that the best calf crop was due to the fastest horse and the longest rope, but there were very few rustlers among the hard-working settlers and most of the killings were unjustified.

The violence that developed led to the hanging of Cattle Kate and Jim Averill. The trial of the murderers was tossed around in the courts and eventually out of them. The State Association recruited a group called the "Invaders," who were hired guns from Texas to fight with members of the big ranch owners' group. After things settled down, members of the Wyoming Livestock Association began to take up homesteads, desert claims, and tree claims. They also bought land in order to get legal pasture for their cattle. However, many of the men on the Invader's "list" like Billy Hill, Ed Starr, Long Henry, and others left Wyoming for Montana because of the very unstable conditions. Other cowboys from small as well as large ranches headed across the border and became part of Montana's open-range crew.

There were over 650,000 cattle trailed from Texas to Montana, largely in 1882 and '83. Here, too, the owners realized that the losses from cattle

Granville Stuart, who organized a Vigilante group in north-central Montana that hanged or shot seventeen of the twenty known cattle thieves and practically put an end to cattle rustling and horse stealing in that area. One rustler escaped, two were shot in Lewistown by a group of alarmed and defensive citizens. Davis, Hauser and Stuart owned the DHS Pool with 25 brands. *Photo courtesy E. H. Train and Montana Historical Society, Helena.*

rustling were increasing at an alarming rate. At the close of the spring roundup of 1884, a few of these Montana stockmen met at the D-S Ranch (later the D.H.S.) decided to take action against the rustlers who were stealing valuable horses as well as an estimated 3 percent of the range cattle.

Under the leadership of Granville Stuart[1], they formed a Vigilance Committee, which came to be known as "Stuart's Stranglers." Soon after this meeting, William Thompson, one of the members of the Stranglers, ran into Narciss LaVardure and Joe Vardner with seven saddle horses that had been stolen from J.A. Wells. In the ensuing shoot-out, Vardner was killed and LaVardure was taken prisoner. He was seized by the armed posse and hanged.

In 1884, Bill McKenzie stole Spud Murphy's blue mare down on the Missouri River and headed for Fort McGinnis sixty miles away. Lee Scott at Rocky Point started out to look for the missing blue mare. Lee and his cowboys caught McKenzie, shot, and wounded him. When he surrendered they hanged him on a big cottonwood tree about one-and-a-half miles below the Fort on Hancock Creek.

Rocky Point was a cluster of adobe-chinked huts built on the cliffs above the Missouri. It had a hotel of sorts and several saloons. It was never a "nice" place, but as the wolfers, trappers, and traders began to leave and the Missouri River boat traffic dwindled, Rocky Point became a hangout for cattle rustlers and tough characters out of a job.

Cattle rustlers were operating openly in the Lewistown area and causing severe losses to the ranchers. The people in that area were ready to take matters into their own hands. On July 4, 1884, two ring leaders of the cattle stealing, Edward "Longhair" Owen and Charles "Rattlesnake" Jake Fallon, described as the most villainous-looking, rode into town. After they had lost all of their money on a horse race and became roaring drunk, they started shooting up the town.

Local citizens armed with Winchester rifles took up positions in the stores and on the roofs along the only street. During the shoot-out that followed, Longhair Owen was critically wounded, so Rattlesnake Jake fought his way back to help his cohort; the two kept firing until they could no longer pull the triggers of their guns. Rattlesnake was hit nine times and Longhair had eleven bullet holes in him. The citizens of Lewistown had formed no posse, but they noisily and thoroughly took care of two of the twenty thieves known to be in that cattle rustling ring.

Soon after that, the livestock owners hanged Billy Downs and "California" Ed at the mouth of the Musselshell River. Members of the Vigilance Committee left for Rocky Point, where they captured Red Mike and Brocky Gallagher—notorious horse thieves—and hanged them. Others from the Vigilance group went down to an unused woodyard at Bates Point, fifteen miles below the Musselshell River, where they had a shoot-out, burned a haystack and cabin, and destroyed the tent of eleven horse thieves. Old Man James, his two sons, and a nephew were shot or burned to death in the cabin. "Stringer" Jack was shot in a dense clump of willows; Dixie Burr, who was Granville Stuart's nephew, had his arm shattered by a rifleball, but he escaped on a raft with Silas Nickerson, Orvil Edwards, and Swift Bill. The four were stopped by soldiers at Poplar Creek Agency on the Missouri and arrested.

A U.S. marshal then started for White Sulphur Springs with the four men, but at the mouth of the Musselshell, Stuart's Stranglers took the four men and hanged them on a log that they put between two cabins.

Paddy Rose, one of the eleven men sought by these vigilantes, hid in a washout in the badlands and made his way to Fort Benton on foot. There, influential relatives helped him escape to Canada.

In all, two thieves were killed by citizens; the Stuart Stranglers shot or hanged seventeen thieves, and only Paddy Rose escaped. The Vigilance posse recovered 284 stolen horses and virtually put an end to the large-scale horse and cattle stealing in much of Montana.

In north-central Montana, a cattle-versus-sheep battle flared briefly. For a short time the sheepmen and the cattlemen were doing some vicious fighting over the open land on which both groups ranged. Asa Gray, a sheepherder for the Long Investment Company of Stanford, had herded sheep in Phillips County near Malta, during the time of this range war between the sheepmen and the cattlemen. Five men came into his sheep camp and shot him in the head and left thinking he was dead. According to Asa, they also shot and killed his two dogs and killed or crippled at least a dozen of his sheep. Asa later proved that he had been shot in the head by showing where the bullet went in and out of the front of his head just above his eyes. It had gone under the skin and along the frontal bones. The owners of the sheep took Asa to a hospital where he completely recovered within a few days. As far as he knew, his assailants were never found or charged with assault.

Animosity remained for a long time between sheepmen and the cattle owners who saw their mountain pastures being close-cropped by bands of sheep. Gradually that, too, has lessened and a cowboy now will even speak to a sheepherder.

The lessons that the big cattlemen in Wyoming learned seem to have been carried over to the livestock industry in Montana as there were no pitched battles between the big cattle pools and the homesteaders.

After a few encounters and the decisive action of Stuart's Stranglers in central Montana, the remaining would-be rustlers decided that kind of crime didn't pay and either left the area or turned to honest work. The problems of the cattle pools were greatly reduced.

As the homesteaders and small ranchers gradually took over most of the choice land, the owners of the large herds of cattle began to take up homesteads and develop their own ranches. The powerful cattle pools were soon a part of history, but they had served a real need in the early days of cattle raising in Montana.

References:
[1] Sandoz, Marie, *The Cattlemen* (Hastings House Pub., NY, 1958), p. 331.

[2] Stuart, Granville, *Journal and Reminiscences*, Vol. II (H.C. Arthur and Co., Glendale, CA, 1957), pp. 195-226 (P.C. Phillips, editor).

KID AMBY CHENEY, RIDER ON THE OPEN RANGE
CHAPTER SIX

" " The settling of the West is our oldest and most enduring legend. It transformed cowboys... into folk heroes and turned villains into national celebrities."[1] During the last decade of the 1800s, people in the Midwest and in the East were caught up in the sheer adventure and challenge offered by the West. The young and adventurous ones made their way to this Western frontier—the others enjoyed it vicariously through stories that drifted back to "the states."

Ambrose Valencourt Cheney was one of the teenagers living in a little Illinois town and dreaming of the exciting life out West. He was determined to get there and finally made it when he was thirteen. His life, adventures, and work in Montana spanned the eras of open ranges for cattle and the homesteading, fencing, and "settling" of the state.

Born in 1874, Ambrose led a normal little boy's life in La Harpe, Illinois, fishing in the river and playing baseball when he and his friends could get the equipment. The boys made their own baseballs, starting with a piece of rubber from an old overshoe, winding string around that, covering it with scraps of leather, and sewing it with beeswax thread. Bats were made by whittling a hardwood stick into the right shape. The players wore knee pants and, when they could get them, their mothers' long black stockings to add an element of style.

Many years later, Amby was to braid his own rawhide ropes for roping cattle on Montana's open ranges and later still he taught his seven sons to play baseball as he had learned it back in La Harpe.

Hezekiah and Phoebe Lincoln were neighbors of the Cheneys in La Harpe. Hez was a nephew of Abraham Lincoln, but he often imbibed too freely. The boys of the neighborhood teased Hez by pulling his coattails as he walked, and down he would tumble. When he started to the saloon one day, it was Amby's turn to pull the tail of Hez's Prince Albert coat. This time Hez reached in his pocket and took out a heavy scale weight, threw it, and hit Amby on the head, fracturing his skull. He was unconscious and in the hospital for a long time and Phoebe Lincoln nursed him back to health. Amby carried a deep scar and depression on the back of his head for the rest of his life.

Amby grew up listening to stories of the Civil War from Linas, his father, who had fought with the Union army, been taken prisoner of war, been released through a North-South exchange, and then re-enlisted to fight the rest of the war. And there was the story of Royce Oatman, a cousin, who had gone West with his family in a covered wagon train. In Arizona they separated from the main contingent and were subsequently ambushed by Indians. Royce, his wife, and one small child were killed. A fifteen-year-old son was left for dead, and the two girls were taken captive by the Indians. (Many years later, the boy, who had been found by another wagon train, rescued his sister, Olive. She wrote a book, *Captivity of the Oatman Girls*, describing their life in the Indian camps and the death of her little sister.)

But all those stories were overshadowed by the ones that were trickling back about the big cattle drives and the cowboys in Montana. Amby and his younger brother, Melvin, longed for a life in that romantic, untamed West.

In 1887, Amby and his friend, Jinx Matthews, ran away from home and headed West. For a time they lived in caves on the bank of the Mississippi River near Burlington, Iowa. From there they went on to Fort Madison hoping to catch a train that would take them to Montana. They were living on hand-outs and sleeping in saw-dust piles to keep warm since it was December and cold. They managed to get on a westbound freight train, but the crew and the police decided the boys should go back to their parents, and they arrived home just in time for Christmas dinner.

Spring came and Amby was more determined than ever to go West, so Perry Westfall and his bride, the former Ella Berges, took Amby, her half-brother, with them as they headed back to their cattle ranch in Montana. It was 1888, and they took a train to Great Falls. From there they took a stage coach to the coal mining town of Belt and on to Armington, Raynesford, and Geyser. When they got to Antelope Buttes, west of Old Stanford, they left the stage and walked two miles south to the Westfall Ranch. This was the Judith Basin and there were three ranches—Bill Skelton's, Bob Skelton's, and Westfall's—all members of the Judith Basin Cattle Pool, which was to play a large part in Amby's life and the realization of his dream to be a Montana cowboy.

Old Stanford with its seven saloons, one hotel, and the Mercantile store was a famous stage stop and their nearest town. Amby did chores on the Westfall ranch and sometimes he took eggs in to the Mercantile and traded them for candy. He listened to the talk of the working cowboys; some of them showed him how to handle a rope and he practiced diligently. One old hand told him he could make his hat brim stiff by putting beef gall on it and ironing it in. His hat was good and stiff until the first rain, and then the beef gall ran down his neck and the hat was droopy again.

Saloon and patrons in Old Stanford, Montana, c. 1899. Far left Melve Cheney; third from right Andy Matthews; second from right Amby Cheney. *Photo courtesy, Robert Gunderson and from the collection of Grace McGiffin, Later Mrs. Melvin Cheney.*

He heard reports of the frequent stagecoach hold-ups around Antelope Buttes and how they finally had to change the route to more open country so the robbers wouldn't have so many hiding places. Adventure was all around him, but so far Amby hadn't been able to get into it.

One day, when he and Weary Willie Skelton didn't have anything to do and no money to go to the store, they caught Will's cousin, Matt Skelton, tied him to a wagon wheel, and rolled him down hill. When Matt hollered, his father, Chambers Skelton, came running and shouting. The two boys took off on a run for Antelope Buttes and hid out until dark, cautiously weighing the possibility of meeting some hold-up men with black handkerchiefs over their faces—against the wrath of Matt's father.

During the spring roundup of '88, Amby was taken out to see the "goings on" as the cowboys were getting ready to go out. "I had just turned fourteen and I cried when they thought I was too young to begin cowboying. I saw a young boy sleeping on a saddle and figured he wasn't much older than I was. This didn't ease my pain in the least."

Amby did get to work some on the fall roundup that year, but he spent the rest of the winter helping on the Westfall Ranch. By then more of his relatives had arrived from Illinois. Amby's mother, Hanoria, had first been married to Hiram Berges and they had five children: Ella, Lena, Lizzie, Bernie, and Girard. Hiram had come to Montana in 1886. By her second marriage to Linas Cheney, Hanoria had two sons, Ambrose and Melvin.

SO LONG COWBOYS OF THE OPEN RANGE

All of them moved to Montana, and in some way, most of them became connected with the cattle industry.

In the spring of 1889, Amby signed on to work full time as a horse wrangler and night-herder with the Judith Basin Pool. He had to get up at 3 or 4 o'clock each morning to get the remuda (horse herd) into the rope corral so each cowboy could choose and rope the horse he was to ride that day. The men were expected to be through with breakfast and ready to ride their circles by daybreak.

As a horse wrangler during those first few years, Amby would often take 200 head of horses and swim them across a high creek or the Judith River in order to get them to good grass. He sometimes had to race with wranglers from other outfits to get his cavy of horses to the best grass.

Because he was the youngest one on the crew, he was called "Kid Amby" by the other cowboys and the name stuck throughout his life.

In the fall of '89, Kid Amby helped move cows and calves, and day-herded cows on the Basin outfit's range. The weaner calves had to be identified and branded to ensure proper ownership. Amby began to learn the brands and to whom they belonged. In later years he was to become an expert on identifying brands and ownership.

It was that first fall, too, when Amby helped herd the cows and calves on the Phillips' ranch. During dinner one day, Mrs. Phillips screamed and ran toward the beaver dams where her children were playing. Amby and the men followed and found that her three-year-old son had fallen into the water. They got him out, tried hot water respiration and every means they knew to revive him, but with no success.

Charlie Russell came to work for the Basin Pool, and for several years he and Amby worked together as horse wranglers and night-herders. "I usually roped Charlie's horse for him. We could never let him in the horse herd because he would swing his rope and scatter the herd and break down the rope corral," Amby explained.

Amby went on to "real" cowboying and eventually became one of the top ropers in the Basin and then the Bearpaw Pool. He also worked as a "rep" for them at other cattle pools. A rep was a cowboy who was sent to ride through neighboring herds to retrieve his outfit's cattle that had gotten mixed in. He had to be observant, quick, and have a good memory and knowledge of brands and owner's names.

Russell went on to become Montana's most famous artist preserving for all time those open range days and the cowboys who rode in them.

Kid Amby had worked for two years for the Judith Basin Pool, and after the fall roundup and cattle shipping he drew his season's pay and headed for the Westfall Ranch where his mother lived with her daughter, Ella, and Perry Westfall. On the way to the ranch, he met some of his cowboy pals, who suggested that they teach him how to play the game of "Three Card Monte." They jerked the saddle off one of the horses and used the saddle blanket for a table. When they finished the game, Amby had no money left. He said that the hardest thing he ever had to do as a cowboy was to go home and tell his mother that he was without any money from his whole summer's wages.

In telling his sons about the old days in the West, Amby said, "Practically all the cowboys wore guns but they surely were not gun-slingers with notches in their guns. Those early cowboys let it be known that they wanted to live. They used their guns mainly to kill rattlesnakes, small game, and the badgers whose holes were a real hazard to running horses. Many a horse got a broken leg and many a cowboy was thrown because his horse stepped in a badger hole. The only time the open range cowboys would shoot at another person was when they were cornered or when there was no other way out of a fracas."

Carrying two guns became a matter of defense as well as style. The way those guns were holstered is shown in the picture of the five cowboys of the Judith Basin Pool (page 23) who went to Fort Benton for their Saturday night action. One of them suggested that they get Dan Dutro, the new photographer in town, to take their picture as long as they were all dressed up. So they got on their horses and away they went, but when they got to town they decided an action picture would be best. They borrowed a milk cow to rope. Al Malison roped the cow and the others got themselves and their ropes, guns, and horses all set so they would show best in the two pictures. George Barrows, Amby Cheney on Old Gene, Al Malison on Antelope, Claude Dowen, and Jack Emerson, on a horse they called "76", were in the two pictures but in different positions.

Back at the roundup camp, the boss was waiting to send the five of them after some Basin Pool cattle. They were to ride along the Missouri River and adjacent breaks where some big steers had escaped the roundups because they were hidden in the coulees and valleys of the breaks.

The cowboys spread out and each one took out after one of those six- or seven-year-old steers. He had to rope the steer, tie him down, and then, taking a small rope from his pocket, tie a cottonwood or very heavy willow pole to the horns of the animal. After the steer hit the brush a few times, he could easily be headed toward the beef herd. Often steers which were herd-quitters would have to be handled in that way or thrown down several times before they would stay in the herd. When asked how they removed the poles from the steers' horns, Amby explained that the poles would move back and forth and wear out the ropes so the poles would fall off.

The older herd-quitting steers kept trying to break away from the beef herd, especially at night. "If the cattle were 'touchy,' " Amby said, "we'd bed them down a mile or so from camp to avoid night noises that might spook them. Those old herd-quitters were ready to start a stampede at the slightest disturbance. In addition to the two regular night-herders, there were often two other guards who worked three-hour shifts in bad weather or when there was a spooky herd of cattle."

If the men were night-herding in an area where there was little wood, every cowboy would use his spare time to fill his saddle bags with buffalo (or cow) chips. It got to be a contest in cold weather to see who could get the most. When the night-herder came in, he would put a supply of chips on the campfire and also in the stove which kept the bed-tent warm so the men could dress and undress in relative comfort.

Accidents did happen and the cowboys did the best they could to meet any emergency. Professional medical help was often fifty or a hundred horseback miles away. Badger holes were a constant danger, and Amby fell victim to one of them. Once when his outfit was just about to finish a roundup job, Amby flushed out a big steer and took after him. Just as he was about to throw a loop, his horse stepped in a badger hole, and Amby was thrown off. His ankle was broken, but he got up and, using his good left leg, managed to get on his horse and make it back to the bed-wagon. The men killed a small steer, skinned it and, supervised by the cook, wrapped strips of green hide around the splints that had been put on his ankle. For more than a month, he hobbled around with the drying leather shrinking to form a perfect cast. In six weeks, he was back at work, good as ever, with the ankle bone knit perfectly in place.

Amby was one of the cowboys who successfully took thousands of cattle across the Missouri River in the summers of 1890 and '91. The Judith Basin Pool was dissolved because so many of the cattle owners that belonged to it took their herds across the river and into the Milk River country. There they reorganized, took in other owners, and formed the Bearpaw Pool. Amby went with them and worked for many years as a rep, riding other ranges to locate and reclaim animals that belonged in the Bearpaw Pool. He knew the brand of every member of the Pool, so he could cut out the strayed animals and bring them back to a holding place and eventually to camp headquarters.

Crossing the Missouri River was dangerous at best, but when it began to ice over in the late fall it was even more treacherous. In 1895, Amby and his friend, Billy Weaver, had finished the fall round-up, drawn their pay, and were ready to go home to the Judith Basin. Amby was anxious to get started, but Billy was having good luck at the gambling tables in Chinook, and besides, he had a girlfriend there and was reluctant to leave. Amby got tired of waiting for his pal to make up his mind, so he finally said, "If you won't go tomorrow, I'll go alone." Billy, trying to dissuade him, said, "We can't start on Friday, that's bad luck."

But Amby persisted and when Friday morning came, the two cowboys started out on horseback for the Missouri River crossing at Clagett. When they got there, they found that the river was icing up and the ferry boat had been taken out for the winter. A rancher who lived on the north bank of the river invited them to stay with him until morning, telling them that a Dutchman who was working for him went across on the ford every morning to cut wood and knew it so well that the cowboys could just follow him across. It was night then, and they were glad to accept the rancher's invitation. After breakfast the next morning, they saddled up their horses and started out across the river following the Dutchman whose horse was old and slow. All went well until suddenly Amby's younger and more spirited horse lunged ahead and was swept off his feet by the current, and he began to drift downstream.

Burdened with a heavy coonskin coat, Amby had to stay with his horse until finally a sharp current swept horse and rider up on a sandbar on the opposite river bank half a mile downstream. It was freezing cold and by the time the shivering cowboy rode over to Bill Norris's store and saloon, his wet clothes had frozen him to the saddle. A man there pried him loose and took him into the store to thaw out. They gave him a dry suit of underwear from the stockpile in the store. Norris put him to bed and fixed a strong drink—a hot toddy it was called when used for medicinal purposes. A day at the Norris home warmed Amby up enough so on Sunday, he put on his own dried-out clothes and rode alone the forty miles to his home at the Westfall Ranch, west of Stanford.

On that Friday, when Billy saw what was happening to Amby, he turned his horse around in midstream and went back to the shore he had left. He decided to ride the hundred miles to Fort Benton and cross the Missouri by bridge.

Winters were tough in Montana and the summers were hot. On one of those hot summer days in the early '90s, a group of Bearpaw Pool cowboys were riding circle out on Sun Prairie, northeast of Harlem. They noticed a bunch of wild horses grazing on the flat. The men didn't pay too much attention to them until someone happened to see that one of the horses had a saddle turned under his belly. Riding up closer, the men saw that the horse's back was covered with saddle sores and it looked as though he had been carrying that saddle for a long time. They decided to rope him and get the saddle off. It wasn't easy, as the horses were wild and fast. After a good many unsuccessful tries at roping, they managed to get the whole herd into a deep coulee. Kid Amby was known as one of the best ropers in the Bearpaw Pool, so they stationed him near the mouth of the coulee while the other fellows held the horse herd, allowing them to come out one at a time...or as near that as possible.

Finally, the horse bearing the saddle came by on the run. Amby swung his rope and front-footed him. The other cowboys jumped on the horse when he fell, tied him down, and took the saddle off. They got the horse back to camp, doctored his sores with axle grease, and turned him loose with the camp herd.

Amby was by then a lanky eighteen-year-old kid so the other cowboys decided he should have the saddle. It was pretty well beaten up but looked better than the old one he was riding. However, the first time he roped a steer from that saddle, the cinch broke and Amby went spinning sky-high and then landed on the ground with a thud.

"After that stray horse's sores got better," Amby recalled, "several of the boys tried to ride him, but he bucked so hard he threw them off one after another, so we gave him up as an outlaw.

"One day Dutch Henry came along and said, 'I'll bet you fellas anything that you want to bet that I can fork* him.'

"We thought we had a cinch, and we pooled all the money in camp and bet that he couldn't ride the outlaw. By this time it was early fall and the mornings were getting pretty cold. But instead of taking advantage of this and making Dutch Henry ride him when the horse was cold and had a hump in his back and could buck like the devil," Amby said when relating the story, "we let Dutch ride him at noon when he was all warmed up and though he really did buck, Dutch managed to stay with that horse and took all our money.

"That left the rest of us dead-broke until payday," Amby continued, "and we were sure sore about it. So we began planning how to get even. The next morning as we started out from camp, Con Price, who was a pretty sharp gambler, winked at me and said, 'Kid, stick close to me on circle today. I want to show you something.' After we had gone a good ways from camp and the sun had begun to warm things up, Con said, 'Here's a good place to let our horses rest.' We threw off our saddles, dropped the reins so the horses wouldn't go far, and spread out our saddle blankets. Then Con got out an old deck of cards and began teaching me how to make a false cut. It took several days of practice before I really mastered the art of making the cut, but when I got it down pat, Con and I got Dutch Henry into a poker game. We really cleaned him and got our money back—with maybe a little interest. We shared our winnings with the other cowboys who had lost money on Dutch Henry's ride."

Later that fall, a couple of Mounties came from Canada and took the outlaw horse back with them, but they didn't bother with the old saddle with a broken tree. The saddle was so battered that they told Amby to keep it as a reward for roping the horse for them. Amby fixed it up the best he could and continued to ride with it. One day when he was riding near Samples Crossing on the Judith River, Amby met old Jess Samples. The two cowhands sat on their horses and visited a little while until the conversation got around to the subject of saddles. Jess, who was riding a saddle with a broken horn, proposed a trade. "How much to boot?" asked Amby, who was a born horse trader. They finally settled on a $10 boot, which Jess handed over promptly, anxious to get rid of his saddle with the broken horn. Jumping off their horses, the men quickly exchanged saddles and Amby, with the $10 in his pocket, threw his newly acquired saddle on his horse, remounted, and rode off as fast as possible.

When Jess put his "new" saddle on his horse, the cantle flapped up against the horn and he realized that the saddle had a broken tree, which made it practically useless. Jess yelled, "Come back here, you damn kid," and Amby heard him swearing as he went over the hill. A trade was a trade—that was the law of the range, so Amby never looked back as he rode on to camp. "Poor old Jess, I never saw him again," mused Amby in later years. "Wonder what ever became of him."

---

* "Fork" meant to ride and stick on a bucking horse.

Amby was famous for his backhand loop in roping any kind of animal. Wild Bill Sutter, a Basin Pool cowboy who became a brand inspector, said he knew of only two men who could throw that loop, so Amby explained how he did it and how he used it to catch that Canadian outlaw horse. "In throwing the backhand loop, I never swing my rope, but with the coil in my left hand and the loop in my right hand, I throw the rope so that the opened loop hits the ground and rolls up against the front of the back legs of a calf or against the front legs of a horse. Then the animal has to step into the loop with both feet and I pull the rope tight and take a couple of dallys around the saddle horn. If the animal is especially large or strong, I take the end of the rope in my left hand and, in addition to the dallys around the horn, I run it around the tightened rope. This makes it easier to hold a big animal, and at the same time, keep my horse turned directly toward the animals. A good rope horse, like my Old Gene, takes this position and always moves the way he should while an animal is being roped, held, or thrown down."

If the horse to be roped was a bucker or partly "broke," he would be front-footed, thrown, and thus man-handled to take some of the fire out of him. But for the horses in the remuda, Amby could catch them by dragging his loop behind him and dabbing it over the head of a horse, then pulling it quickly so that the loop tightened just behind the ears of the horse.

The cowboys used those roping skills in another area, too. One of the major sports and unofficial assignments was roping wolves, and Kid Amby said, "We did a lot of it." Since the buffalo and other game animals were almost all gone, the wolves were forced to prey on domestic livestock for their food. Wolves would usually run in pairs or even in packs and chase a cow or steer in a circle—with one wolf at the head of the animal and two or more at the rear. Old-timers had the idea that wolves would always ham-string their prey, cutting the rear tendons above the joint, but later kills revealed that the wolves used their sharp teeth to cut off the ears and tail. They slashed, like you would with a butcher knife, up and down along the neck and rear end of the victim. When they got an animal down, the wolves might eat a lot or just pull some of the entrails out of the belly of the cow, eat those, and then go on to another kill.

The Shonkin outfit paid a $5 bounty for each wolf killed and some of the other outfits began offering bounties, so a cowboy could, by roping and killing two or three wolves a month, add $15 or $20 to his monthly $40 paycheck.

According to Amby, full-grown wolves could only be roped when they were full of meat from a kill, so the cowboys watched for wolves at a carcass and for young wolves who were clumsy and just learning to run fast. A cowboy had to have a fast rope horse and one that would not spook when his rider hooked onto a wolf. The men found that some horses were so frightened by a wolf on the rope that they would buck and throw the rider or get the rope tangled up in the brush. If that happened the cowboy would have to cut the rope and let the wolf go.

Roped wolves were killed with a "45" revolver or dragged to death. Roundup bosses didn't get after their cowboys for roping wolves because they recognized wolves as more devastating to their cattle herds than the Indians who often demanded "toll" in cattle for crossing their land.

According to Edward Curnow[2], who made an extensive study of the eradication of the wolves in Montana, the cattlemen deliberately over-estimated in 1878 when they reported that wolves killed 50,000 head of cattle in Montana in one year. The owners wanted the state government to put a bounty on wolves, and they were successful. In 1896 there were 5,866 wolf skins presented for bounty payments and in 1897 it had dropped to 4,495. From '98 on, the number of bounties claimed decreased rapidly. As late as the 1920s, renegades such as the White Wolf of the Judith Basin killed some $15,000 worth of livestock. By then Amby was a rancher with a cattle herd of his own and the famous White Wolf was killing his stock. He took his hound dogs and trailed that wolf on several occasions, but it was a neighbor who finally got it and brought the hide in to be mounted and displayed in the Judith Basin County Courthouse. Three Toes in southeastern Montana was reputed to have killed $50,000 worth of livestock.

Amby never lost his roping skill. He used it on his own cattle ranch and at age eighty-four, he saddled up his horse and went to help a neighboring rancher on branding day. He roped 346 calves without a single miss. That would have been an outstanding feat for a young man and an almost unheard of accomplishment for a man of eighty-four. "Some of you youngbloods better be practicing up and get the hang of this ropin'; I'm not going to last forever, you know," Amby was heard to remark as he unsaddled.

Back in 1902, Amby was still riding bucking horses. One Sunday, when Old Stanford was still a gathering place for cowboys, Amby forked a horse that the assembled cowhands said couldn't be ridden. He scratched the horse with his spurs and finished the ride to the cheers of onlookers who then passed the hat to give him a reward. The collection of $65 was given to Kid Amby—the most money he had ever had together at any one time.

Old Stanford finally gave way to Dubuque, a few miles to the east, where the railroad had established a station. The name of the Dubuque station and post office was later changed to "Stanford."

Charlie Russell and Amby Cheney worked together in both the Judith Basin Pool and the Bearpaw Pool. They remained life-long friends, often meeting in Great Falls during the later years. When Wallace McCracken was gathering material for his definitive work, *The Charles M. Russell Book*[3], he came to Stanford to interview Amby. Nearly seventy years had passed since this "lean old rawhide had shared chuckwagon grub and followed cattle drives with the eccentric young painter." McCracken commented that Kid Amby remembered those days well and that he had never left the old Judith Basin range. He quoted Amby's description, "The

"Painting the Town" by Charles Russell. "Wild Bill" Sutter remembered the incident that inspired the picture and identified the man with the rope as Kid Amby cheney. *Photo courtesy of Range Riders Museum, Miles City, Montana.*

first time I worked with Charlie Russell was on the Judith roundup...over at Old Utica. I was just a kid, but Charlie was the sort of character you don't forget. He was the queerest sort of cowboy I'd ever seen. A homely awkward cuss—all his clothes looked like they'd been junked by some reservation half-breed. Even his face looked like he had some Injun blood in him. A big brimmed hat didn't have any crown or shape to it—like he'd slept in it many a rainy night on the range. His leather pants had seen the last of their second-best days—one leg tucked in a boot and the other hangin' out like a squaw dress. At first I figured he was just a no-good drifter who'd dropped in for a free feed, but it didn't take long to see that he was really one of the bunch and stood damn well with the best of 'em.'' McCracken wondered if the character Amby was describing could possibly have been one of those rough riding cow punchers of the open range days. He pressed Amby to give an opinion and after hedging a bit, Amby explained, "He was no roughrider at all. Charlie was always afoot in the saddle when it came to real cowpunching.'' Then Kid Amby quickly added, with a sparkle coming into his grayed eyes and a smile spreading over his wrinkled face, "But don't get me wrong, he was one of the swellest guys I ever knew. Everybody liked Kid Russell. Sure, he wasn't even a good night-herder. About all he could do was tell stories and make little sketches of the funny things that happened. We'd hurry in at night, just to listen to his yarns and laugh at the pictures he drew. Nobody ever thought he'd amount to anything. But Charlie had lots of friends. And there wasn't a cattle outfit, big or small, that wouldn't hire him. He helped keep us happy."

Later in the conversation after Bess, his wife, had gone out of the room, Amby made a slight correction. "There was one time when Charlie could ride like hell. That was when we came to town, to have a few drinks, and to see the girls. There was nobody in the outfit that could beat Kid Russell to the front door of the hottest places in town."

Amby remembered that on Saturday nights, he often teamed up with Russell and others to provide music for the country dances. Amby played his harmonica or chorded on the piano, if one were available. Charlie played the comb with a cigarette paper over it, or for a bass stroked a broom handle in the rosin on the dance floor. If Mexican Joe was around, there was guitar music, too.

Russell married Nancy, moved to Great Falls, and settled down to a life of serious painting.

After fourteen years of cowboying for the Basin and Bearpaw pools, Amby left that work and became a jerk-line freighter. A typical freight outfit consisted of twelve to fourteen horses pulling up to three wagons and a small caboose in which the driver could eat and sleep. Sometimes Amby had a saddle horse tied behind the caboose. The lead horse was driven with a single line, and a jerk on this line with a "gee" called out made him turn right, while a "haw" and jerk on that line would turn him and, therefore, his teammates to the left. The horses were reined to one another so they followed the lead horse. A driver often got out and walked beside the wheel or just behind the rear horse. If he saw a rough pull ahead, he might even ride the left wheel horse and throw a small rock to wake up any horse that was not pulling his share of the load.

At night the outfit could stop any place there was good feed for the horses. Amby hobbled his saddle horse and kept him nearby so he could get the others into a rope corral in the morning. Hopefully he could get the fourteen horses harnessed and on the road by daybreak.

Amby freighted out of Fort Benton where the river boats unloaded supplies for the whole state. Cargoes usually consisted of staples that would travel well—like sugar, flour, salt, cereals, beans, and canned fruits and vegetables. Amby hauled for the store and stations through the Judith Basin and to Armington and Lewistown.

The harshness of the frontier often took its toll, and Amby came upon one of its tragedies as he was driving his freight team and wagons over Arrow Creek hill north of Stanford. There was a lone covered wagon and in the driver's seat a strange and dejected-looking man. Amby sensed something was wrong, and he could see that the man's horses were about played out. He stopped to talk to the driver and learned that the man had become so discouraged with homestead farming that he had killed

A real jerkline freight team, note the fourteen horses, caboose, and saddle horse. This is the William I. Hughes outfit. Kid Amby Cheney freighted with Hughes and had an outfit just like this one. *Photo courtesy of Gerald and Harley Hughes.*

his wife and three children. So Amby went on to Stanford and got word to the sheriff to come get the man and the bodies of his family.

On another trip, Amby had just gotten up the Arrow Creek Hill, unhitched, and fed his horses when he saw a stray buckskin horse at the feed rack with them. Every driver carried oats for his teams, and fed them night and morning. When Amby pulled out the next morning, the buckskin followed his freight outfit. On the third day of that trip, one of Amby's horses got sick, so he caught the stray buckskin and put him in the harness for a replacement. Evidently, the stray had been trained as part of a freight outfit because he fit right in and pulled his share of the load. Amby named him Smoky and eventually he became the lead horse and responded immediately to the jerk line and commands of "gee" and "haw."

On occasions, when there was excessive mud or snow on a hill, Amby would have to unhook the wagons and take them one at a time to the top of the hill.

Amby stayed with freighting full time until the railroads came in and took over the hauling, but even after he had settled on a homestead, he sometimes freighted to get money for the cattle he needed to buy to stock his ranch. Smoky and several horses from his freighting string were taken to the homestead. This was the beginning of the horse herd that was to be an important factor in running the ranch. Horses furnished all workpower and transportation for many years. Cars and tractors came much later.

It was around 1901 when Amby Cheney took up a homestead on Surprise Creek and also filed on a "tree claim." By planting trees on two sides of a square of land, one could claim that area. The land was in what was then Cascade County but with later divisions became Judith Basin County. He and his brother, Melvin, and half-brother, Girard Berges, cut logs from the timber on Dry Wolf Creek and built a fourteen-foot by sixteen-foot cabin. Clear, sparkling, fish-filled Surprise Creek ran through the property some sixty feet from the house. As they put the last sod on the roof and set up a stove with a chimney, the three brothers stood back and admired their cabin. It was to be their home for several years. It wasn't fancy, but it was a shelter, and they owned it.

Girard was soon to file on land farther up the creek and build his own cabin. In 1903, Amby and Melve began renovating the sod-roofed cabin. They pasted fresh newspapers over the inside log walls, added some store-bought furniture, and even washed the windows because Amby was courting the schoolmarm down at Westfall's.

Elizabeth McGiffin had completed a year of study at St. Vincent's Academy in Helena, passed the state examinations, and was awarded a teaching certificate. Perry and Ella Westfall had requested a teacher for their daughter, Nora, and Elizabeth took the job. She came by stagecoach from Great Falls on a cold, snowy December day. The driver changed horses at the stations in Box Elder, Belt, and in Cora Creek, where the travelers were served a good hot dinner. (In Montana, dinner is the noon meal and supper is what you eat in the evening.) The stagecoach travelers continued on through the afternoon to Geyser and finally to Old Stanford arriving there long after dark. The only lights to greet them were the ones in the seven saloons and the Mercantile store. It seemed that was all there was to the town, but finally the stage pulled up in front of the old log hotel and the passengers went into the dining room for a late supper. Elizabeth was the only female on the stage with six or seven men who had been very kind and courteous to her all day, but as she entered the dimly lit dining room, she felt very strange and lonely. She was seventeen years old and had spent the past four years in fairly large towns. Just as she was considering whether it would be best to remain on the stage and travel all night to Lewistown and then return to Great Falls where her family lived, Mrs. Andy Matthews, the proprietor's wife, came into the dining room and took the young girl under her wing. Elizabeth was reassured and decided to stay in Stanford to teach, little dreaming that this area would be her home for over seventy years.

The next morning the sun was shining on the snow and a man from the Westfall Ranch came to get her. Thus she began her teaching career as a private tutor to Nora Westfall. Elizabeth, who came to be known as "Bess," taught at the ranch all winter and was "keeping company" with Kid Amby. For a summer job she went to Highwood, where the people had just built a schoolhouse and had enough money to pay a teacher for three months. There were eighteen pupils, some older than she was. On weekends she and a friend, who had a teaching job at a nearby country school, rode into Great Falls. Each of the girls had bought a horse for $25 and a saddle for another $25. They made the thirty-mile ride to town on Friday and back on Sunday. They attended dances in the schoolhouses. Kid Amby always showed up to escort Bess when there was a dance scheduled. But cowboys were so plentiful and girls so scarce that it was kind of an unwritten law of the range that every man there got to dance with at least one girl during the evening—sometimes that took until well into the morning hours. To compensate for the dearth of ladies, some of the cowboys tied handkerchiefs around their arms to indicate they would be dancing the woman's part in the "squares."

When the Highwood term ended, Bess went over to teach another three months at the Buckland School, three miles above the present town of Highwood, at a salary of $50 a month. There she had seven pupils, all of them small, as the big boys were then working in the fields. Bess had to saddle four or five horses each afternoon for the children. Some of them rode double and only Alfred Buckland, who was thirteen, could saddle his own horse.

By the end of the term, Amby and Bess had decided to get married and had set December as the time.

Bess had come from a pioneering family that came to Montana in 1882 and settled in the Stockett-Sand Coulee area. She was the first white girl born in that section of Montana. It was 1885 and there was only a little settlement at the place that was later to become Great Falls. Her father, Nat McGiffin, had tried cattle raising, but most of his herd died in the severe winters of '82 and '83. He trailed sheep in from Deer Lodge, but a blizzard killed them all. The fine horses that he had shipped out by freight train from Iowa got into the loco weed and by spring all but one mare was useless.

Elizabeth's mother, May Junkin McGiffin, had books and a little piano sent out from Iowa and she taught her five children at home. But when Elizabeth was twelve, May died, so Nat sent Elizabeth and her younger sister, Grace, and the three boys back to their Junkin grandparents in Fairfield, Iowa. Elizabeth took the four-year high school course in three years and by the time she graduated, the grandparents were no longer able to care for all those children, so Nat brought them back to Great Falls and made a home for them there.

Now Elizabeth was eighteen and she had fallen in love with a cowboy, Kid Amby Cheney. He was twenty-nine.

It was another cold and snowy winter day when the young couple were married at noon on December 15, 1903, in Great Falls. Amby had a new buggy with red wheels, and they left immediately for the long, tedious trip over snowy roads to their ranch home at the foot of Wolf Butte. On the first day out they met a car on the Belt Hill. Amby's team reared up in fright and started to run from that noisy "gasoline buggy." It was the first car either the horses or the passengers in the buggy had ever seen and only Amby's driving skill, learned on the freight wagons, kept the team in control and got them all back on the road.

It took two-and-a-half days to make the sixty-mile trip. Bess wrote an account of their arrival and that first cabin home:

It was long past dark when we finally reached the ranch. The little log house looked like a haven of rest. With gay bright wallpaper on the walls, the floor covered with shining linoleum, and new furniture which had been laboriously hauled by wagon from Great Falls. It looked like a small dream home to me. Best of all there was a warm fire glowing in the new range and a hot supper prepared by the men was waiting for us.

I soon learned that love in a cottage isn't all charm and romance. The bright new wallpaper was pasted on a lining of unbleached muslin, which in turn was tacked to rough lumber boards which covered the log walls. I was to learn later that howling winter winds would bring in cold and dust that seeped through every crevice in the unplastered walls and around doors and windowsills.

The cabin had just one room, but Bess partitioned it off with bedsheets to create bedrooms. And she made Amby and Melve take all the empty whiskey bottles off the sod roof.

Their first and second sons were born while they lived in the cabin. In 1907, the men built a big square log house containing a large bedroom and a living/dining area. The Higgin's cabin was moved down and put near the main house. This was made into a kitchen and most meals were eaten there. A connecting hallway supplied a place to hang coats and line up the cowboy boots. Three more sons and a daughter arrived. With each new baby, Elizabeth stacked one more orange crate on those that held the children's clothes.

That log house served the ever-expanding family until 1915, when Amby hired a carpenter with whom he built a big, square, two-story, ten-room house and painted it white. There was an attic and a basement and a big front porch. Two more sons were born in that house.*

Amby and his brother, Melvin, were then running cattle together on their Surprise Creek Ranch in the Judith Basin where a few years before, the Montana cattle industry had thrived on its open ranges. Now it had settlers and fences, so only the mountain pastures were still open land.

Melvin married Elizabeth's sister, Grace, and they, too, came to live on the ranch. Their five children grew up with those of Amby and Bess. It was the era when many sons were an economic bonus on a ranch. The two men and their nine sons did all the outside ranch work. Amby's years as an open range cowboy taught him skills he could transfer to managing his own cattle herd, and he passed the skills with varying degrees of success to those boys of varying ages, aptitudes, and enthusiasm.

They moved a little log schoolhouse onto the ranch and Bess taught all of her children, as well as the nieces, nephews, and Finnish neighbors

*For a detailed account of growing up in a large family on a remote Montana ranch, read *Ranching in the Shadow of Wolf Butte* by Truman M. Cheney.)

Amby and Elizabeth Cheney's seven sons, Roy, Charles, Bernard, Bill, Ambrose Jr., Truman, Thomas, and daughter, May.

all through grade school. Sometimes her $100-a-month salary from the county was all that carried the family through lean years.

When it looked like sheep, with two crops—lambs and wool—would be more profitable than cattle, Amby tried that. He ran sheep for several years, but his heart was never in it. Kid Amby was a cowboy and a cowman and the love of that life lasted through his ninety years.

References:
[1] Lamb, David, "True West," *Missoulian*, Missoula, MT, May 22, 19??, p. A-1.

[2] Curnow, Edward E., *The History of the Eradication of the Wolf in Montana* (Master of Arts thesis, U. of Mont., 1969).

[3] McCracken, Harold, *The Charles M. Russell Book* (Doubleday & Co., Garden City, NY, 1957), pp. 13-14.

[4] Cheney, Truman M., *Ranching in the Shadow of Wolf Butte, The History of a Pioneer Montana Family* (Polebridge Press, Bonner, MT, 1984).

CON PRICE, RIDER OF THE ROUGH STRING
CHAPTER SEVEN

Con Price was a rider of the "rough string" for many cattle outfits in Montana including the Basin and Bearpaw Pools.

He was born in Iowa in 1867 and two years later came to Deadwood, South Dakota, with his parents.[1] As a young teenager, he worked close-herding some cows for a man named Finnegan, and it was then that he got the urge to become a cowboy. In 1885, Con got his first job as a real cowboy with the "7D" outfit on the Belle Forche River in the Black Hills where he night-herded the horses. There were twenty outfits working together employing about 300 cowboys in the cattle pool.

In 1886, Price helped gather and take a herd of cattle from the Black Hills to Miles City and to the "54" Ranch on Mizpah Creek. For most of the following year, Con worked as a bullwhacker on a freight wagon hauling supplies in and out of Wyoming. His real introduction to cowboying was in 1887, when he went to work for the "RL" outfit of the Ryan Brothers on the Musselshell River in Montana. The cowboys were given the job of taking 5,000 head of beef cattle across the Yellowstone River. It took four days because the animals refused to go into the water until the men held them off drinking water and got them so thirsty, they plunged into the river when they were allowed near it. After they were across the river, the men grazed the cattle, moving them very slowly in order to fatten them.

One night, Con got in the middle of a stampede when a horse pulled his picket pin loose and tore through the herd, dragging the rope and picket pin. It was only after the frightened horse got to the other side of the herd that the cowboys were able to get the cattle settled down.

The cattle were sold on the Sioux Indian Reservation in North Dakota. An army officer would allot each steer to a group of Indian families and let them divide it. Previous to this the officer passed on a bunch of cattle and then called five or six Indians with rifles to get up on the fence and shoot the whole bunch before any one of the steers was butchered. In

Con Price and Charlie Russell at their cattle ranch c. 1890. *Photo courtesy of Montana Historical Society, Helena.*

about two hours, according to Con's recounting, there wouldn't be even a tail of a steer left as each family took its share and went back to their campground.

The three chiefs who were at the encampment were Sitting Bull, Rain in the Face, and Gall. Con remembered that Sitting Bull was young and looked as though he had white blood in his veins. Gall and Rain in the Face were old, seasoned warriors and both had been wounded in wars. Rain in the Face, who had planned the Custer Massacre, made a big speech every time a beef was divided and each time the Indians applauded loudly.

After the beef delivery, the men took the cow horses to Mandan, North Dakota, and shipped them back to Montana. The twenty cowboys got on the passenger train and kept the train crew busy trying to keep them in line. Some of the cowboys went on to Texas but Con and the others returned to the RL Ranch. They had one good night's sleep and then started out on the roundup. On the way, they met a man named George Shepherd who said he had been playing poker with a guy named Matt. When Matt reached for a $20 gold piece on the table, an argument ensued and George shot him. George had been working for the RL outfit, so the boss urged him to give himself up, and he was cleared on the grounds of self-defense. Con Price told of another killing on the ranch over a gallon of whiskey.

In the spring of 1890, Con went to work as rough string rider for the TL outfit owned by McNamar and Broadwater. At their ranch near the Bearpaw Mountains, he met up with his old friends, Charlie Russell and Kid Amby Cheney.

Cowboys had to prove themselves with every new outfit they went to work for. When Con arrived at the TL ranch, he was given a horse named "Humpy" and told to try him out. The boss and the other cowboys stood around waiting for action. Con got on the horse, hit him with his hat and spurs, and in a split second landed on the ground a few feet in front of the boss. The men said nothing but the looks on their faces told Con he'd better make good with that horse, so he got on again, spurred Humpy, held on, and galloped off down the road.

Another horse named "Sy" was an outlaw and had thrown several good riders. The boss didn't really want Con to tackle him but consented when the new cowboy said Sy looked like a plowhorse to him. Con got on, scratched the horse with his spurs, and rode him to a finish, later admitting that he was just lucky that day and never rode that horse again. After breaking thirty head of colts, Con quit the job at the TL.

The Milk River range bordered on Canada and the Canadian cattlemen protested the American cattle ranging over and eating their grass. An agreement was made that line riders would be put at all the mounted police camps. These camps were then twenty to thirty miles apart and the plan was looked upon as a joke by the big outfits in north-central Montana. They would take twenty or thirty men and their wagons through or near the Port of Entry and declare they were going to round up all the American cattle. The cowboys did actually gather up several thousand head and report that to the Mounties. Then they would take the herd three or four miles from the border, brand the calves, send the beef steers to Malta or Chinook, and then leave the cows and calves there. In a few days they would be back eating Canadian grass. Con was one of the line riders and was given orders to give the Mounties any amount of beef they wanted to butcher, but the riders and the Royal Canadian Mounted Police both knew that with vast areas of open range and no fences, it was impossible to keep cattle from straying across the border.

In a land where hospitals or even physicians were hundreds of miles apart, cowboys had to help each other. Con went to work for T.C. Powers' Horseshoe Bar Ranch in the Judith Basin. When he arrived at the home ranch, he found that the whole crew had gone off to the fall roundup—all but one very sick man who had been left behind. Con gave him some medicine and sent word to a doctor who came to the ranch and together, they saved the man's life. Soon after that, Con caught up with the roundup crew and was assigned to the night-herding. It was fall and the nights were long and cold.

Camp cooks were notoriously grumpy, if not down-right cantankerous. Big Nose George, the cook here, was no exception, but the two night-herders bravely asked for a lunch and even suggested he might make a pie for them. George glared and said, "Yes, I'll give you a pie." It looked good when George handed them a pie along with their lunch as the two men left for their night-herding job. Hours later when they sat down to eat it, the men found that under the crust was a filling of potato peelings, onion skins, and other scraps. Their first thought was to go back to camp and hit George over the head with it, but then they thought it would be more fun to make the cook eat it. When they rode into camp in the morning, the cowboys were anxious to find out how they felt about what George had put in the pie. Con and his partner unsaddled and went directly to the cook tent. Con had the pie in his hand and George started for him with a butcher knife, but the night-herders jumped on him and got him on the ground. They pried open his mouth and forced the cook to eat a big bite of his pie. When Big Nose George got up, he reached for a neck yoke but Con's partner stuck a Colt 45 in his belly so fast that George threw the neck yoke away and yelled, "Don't kill me."

One of those unwritten laws of the range was that you didn't ask special favors of a camp cook but another one proved just as strong. You couldn't play a dirty trick on a cowboy or push him too far or you'd end up with a Colt 45 in your belly. After the pie episode, things quieted down in the Horseshoe Bar camp. Meals and sack lunches were as usual.

The Horseshoe Bar cowboys rounded up the beef cattle and drove them to Big Sandy. There were two other outfits in town with cattle ready to ship, so Con and his co-workers had to hold the animals there for two days waiting for more stock cars to come in on the railroad. They put in the time drinking and fighting with a bunch of half-breed Indians who had been gathering buffalo bones and had come to town to ship them. Beef was big business and there were several Commission men there trying to get the different cattle outfits to ship to their particular company. The cowboys played cards in the saloons and every once in a while shot off their guns just to keep in practice. One Commission man was lighting his cigar as a shot sounded and his match went out. Charlie Russell, who was standing by, said, "Sir, I saw that bullet go right by your nose." The midwestern Commission man declared he was through playing cards with that bunch—things were getting too rough. That same night, someone stole Con's saddle right off his horse, leaving him afoot, but Charlie said he would go look for it and after following a fresh trail found it cached in the box elder grove.

For a brief period, Con quit cowboying and joined the gold rush to Cripple Creek, Colorado. He soon decided that the mining town was too rough for him, so he came back to Helena, found Russell, borrowed some money from him, and went to work for the D.H.S. outfit near Shelby, where Teddy Blue Abbot was repping. Later Con was sent to Malta to break the rough string for that company, and he had Red Neck Davis as a helper.

In 1896 the D.H.S. was "cleaning up" their Malta range with a view to leaving that part of the country. Con Price and Tom Daly were assigned to work as reps with the different outfits having cattle in that area—among them the Bearpaw Pool, Circle C, Circle Diamond, the Square, and the TL. Here he again met his friend, Kid Amby Cheney, who was repping for the Bearpaw Pool.

Con and Tom helped round up all the D.H.S. cattle and among them found several twelve- or thirteen-year-old steers that had evaded all previous roundups. They put up a fight, and Con won the battle with one of them only after he threw the animal to the ground and broke off one of his horns. As S. Omar Barker[2] described the longhorns:

> He trod out countless cattle trails to mark a frontier's
> dawn,
> Till plows and rails and fences come along to shove him
> on.
> You ask me, "What's a longhorn?" Well, just one more
> word's enough:
> "The longhorn made the cowboy—and he made him
> plenty tough!"

Daniel Floweree came up the trail from Texas in 1873 with a herd of 1,500 longhorns and a year later brought in another bunch from Oregon. He and a partner named Lowery established the F Triangle Ranch with headquarters on Sun River and a range that stretched from the Rockies as far east as Malta. Dutch Herman was the foreman and with Sam Dennison ran the spread for several years.

Besides the story of the one-to-one encounter with the wily thirteen-year-old steer, Con Price, like the other cowboys, entertained around the campfires with lively and occasionally factual stories.

> Now cowboys 'round the fire at night,
> They tell it wide and high.

And one that Con liked to tell was about the time when he was working for the HD outfit that was owned by men from Great Falls, Helena, and Cascade. Jack Lynch was the foreman. "After dinner that night," starts out Con, "we all went to the bunkhouse and the boss brought in a new Winchester rifle to show to the boys. There were ten or twelve of us crowding around the boss to admire his new gun." Next to horses, guns were the most important part of western life. "Someone said, 'Look out. It might be loaded,' and as the inspection went on, it was warned again

'Be sure the damn thing isn't loaded.' " Con was sitting on his bed and thought of the 45 he had under his pillow, so he decided to have some fun with the boys. He shot into the floor of the bunkhouse. "It made a noise like a cannon and poured out a lot of smoke, and every last cowboy tore out of the bunkhouse figuring the Winchester really had been loaded." Con fell back on his bed laughing as he heard one guy shout, "I told you the damn thing might be loaded." When the men finally realized where the shot had come from, they looked in the bunkhouse and figured that if Con hadn't committed suicide, he must at least have gone crazy because he was swinging the gun around as if he might shoot again at any minute. When Con heard this he put the gun back under his pillow and stepped outside. The men looked very serious and then started kidding each other about the whole thing. The boss said he wasn't too sure but that Con was a little bit crazy.

Another one of Con's stories was about old Charlie Bowlegs, who worked for the TL and had notches in his gun. One was for a fellow he killed at Sun River Crossing. Con and Bowlegs drifted into a saloon where Chinaman John hung out. The Chinaman and the house man suggested the boys join them in a poker game. So they played and finally a $50 pot came up. "Bowlegs had a good hand, so he bet all of his money, but before that Chinaman put his money in the pot, he stalled around and stretched his neck to see the top card on the deck as I was dealing. Bowlegs figured there was something wrong, so he said 'Wait a minute, I want to cut the deck.' " The Chinaman and the house man said he couldn't do that. Bowlegs got out his six-shooter and stood up saying that was the way it was going to be. The house man said he'd go behind the bar and get the book of Hoyle to settle the argument. "You stay here," said Bowlegs, "My six-gun is the book of Hoyle in this game, and there's only one way to settle this. We will have Con deal that card to the Chinaman. If it helps his hand, I'm going to take the money. If it doesn't help his hand, and he has the best cards, he can take the money." Since there was really no choice in the face of a loaded six-gun, they agreed. Con dealt the card, and it made the Chinaman two pair so Bowlegs, still holding his gun, raked in the money. They put up a big argument but Bowlegs shoved the pile of chips to the house man and ordered, "Give me the money and do it damn quick." Then Chinaman John's eyes looked like two burnt holes in a blanket. Just before they walked out the door, Bowlegs turned to him and said, "No ketch 'em this time, John."

Con Price and Kid Amby worked or repped for several outfits during the open range days. The Circle Diamond was head-quartered in the Little Rockies. It was also known as the Bloom Cattle Company and its operations were around the town of Malta. The Square outfit belonging to Millner was located between the Milk and Missouri Rivers neighboring on the Bearpaw Pool range. Bill Jaycock was their foreman. The TL outfit belonged to McNamar and Broadwater and was based at a ranch in the Bearpaw Mountains. Sam Miller ran the TL for many years, and Marlow replaced Broadwater as an owner. After they bought the ST from Sands and Taylor and the C2 outfit, the TL became one of the biggest outfits in the area.

The Horseshoe Bar Ranch on Warm Spring Creek in the Moccasin Range was owned by T.C. Powers who had stores at Clagett, Lewistown, and Utica. Bill Deaton was the boss of that outfit.

The D.H.S. outfit, originally put together by Davis, Hauser, and Stuart was first based around Fort Maginnis and then spread to the Judith Basin. Eventually they had two outfits, one at Rock Ridge northwest of Shelby and close to the Canadian border and the other one near Malta on the Milk River. Jim Spurgeon was the D.H.S. boss for many years. Subsequent owners were Reece Anderson, who operated it for some time with Granville Stuart, and then it was taken over by Kohrs, Bielenberg, and Boardman. Teddy Blue Abbot, who married one of Granville Stuart's daughters, was a rep for the D.H.S.

The Half Circle Block outfit was located on the Judith River and was owned by Eastern investors. Tom McShane was the foreman or roundup boss.

The Circle outfit on the Marias River was owned by men living in Fort Benton and Helena. Frank McGuire was the roundup boss.

The PT, located near Havre, was owned by Simon Pepin and Colonel Broadwater of Helena. Sleepy Tom was the foreman. He weighed 240 pounds, had an oversized saddle, and a string of big saddle horses. Tom was sensitive about his size, but his nickname came from the fact that whenever he finished a job, he laid down right there and went to sleep. One time Tom helped unharness the bed-wagon team and as he pulled the last harness off, he laid down by the harness and went to sleep. Just then a rep from the TL outfit came to camp, caught his saddle horse, and was leading him to the tent where he would leave his bed-roll. He saw Tom lying down among the harness and said, "My God, what happened? Did you fellows kill a horse?" Sleepy Tom never liked that rep after that and said he'd be damn glad when that rep cut out his horses and went home to the TL.

Sleepy Tom was big, but he couldn't compare to Baldy Buck, who weighed over 300 pounds. Baldy was an unusual cowboy; he had to have a huge fat-man's saddle and an extra-large horse so he could ride circle. He moved his string of horses from one outfit to another, and it looked like teams of work horses. As he moved from one camp to the other, he could be recognized a long way off—the huge man looming into sight over a hill and then the string of heavy horses—unlike the hundreds of slim, agile cow ponies used by most cowboys.

Bob Malone was foreman of the Bar Eleven and Wallace Taylor ran the ST brand near Choteau.

In later years, the Circle Diamond turned loose 5,000 head of Arizona yearlings on their Milk River range. The cattle kept ranging north until some of them were 200 miles into Canada. In 1897, the range boss sent twenty men with horses, bed wagon, and chuck wagon to look for some of their cattle. Win Cooper, a Texan, was in charge of the Circle Diamond outfit. Some of the stray cattle had gotten as far as Moose Jaw, Saskatchewan, and Con found several D.H.S. steers that were thirteen years old and had come up with a bunch of Arizona cattle. As long as there were open ranges, keeping Montana cattle on this side of the border was a problem.

Each of those early-day cattle outfits ran between 10,000 and 30,000 head of cattle. They had one, two, or three wagons and employed twenty to thirty cowboys. The Bearpaw Pool had about fifty-five brands, thirty-five cowboys, and three or four wagons. According to Con Price, the reps for this pool had a real job and had to be experts on brands. Price felt that repping for a twenty-seven brand outfit was tough enough and said that any rep for the Bearpaw Pool had to have a real good memory for their forty-five brands and keep his eyes open all the time. Kid Amby was one of those Bearpaw Pool reps.

In 1899, Con Price married Claudia Toole, and they settled on land at the head of Kicking Horse Creek in the Sweetgrass Hills. Russell and Con formed a partnership and Charlie and Nancy took up an adjoining home-stead. They had 300 head of cattle branded with a T, which had been Governor Toole's brand. The partners sold out to Peter Wagner, so Price and Russell were out of the cattle business. Charlie settled in Great Falls and preserved for all time with his paintings the spirit of those open range days. Con and Claudia settled in California far from the open ranges of their earlier days.

The names of those open range cattle owners continued to make history in Montana as they often became wealthy businessmen and political leaders.

References:
[1] Price, Con, *Trails I Rode* (Trail's End Pub. Co., Pasadena, CA, 1947).
[2] Price, Con, *Memories of Old Montana* (Trail's End Pub. Co., Pasadena, CA, 1945).
[3] Barker, Omar S., *Rawhide Rhymes* (Doubleday & Co., Garden City, NY, 1968), p. 38.

TEDDY BLUE ABBOTT, DELICATE LITTLE ENGLISH BOY—MONTANA COWBOY
CHAPTER EIGHT

Teddy Blue Abbott, the "delicate" little English boy who was sent West for his health, proved it was a good prescription. He became one of the best of the open range cowboys, driving the trail herds, riding circle and repping for some of the biggest cattle outfits in Montana, drinking hard liquor, and finally marrying the boss's daughter.

Born in Norfolk County, England, in 1860, Teddy came to America with his family in 1871. They settled near Lincoln, Nebraska, but Mr. Abbott and Teddy immediately left for Texas to buy and bring back a herd of longhorns. Teddy's job was to wrangle the horses for the cattle drive. After they got the cattle to the Red River, Mr. Abbott left for Lincoln and Sam Bass, the wagon boss, was left in charge of the drive.

Sam got the longhorns delivered in Lincoln, but eleven-year-old Teddy was soon to learn about the "badmen" of the West, because their trusted wagon boss turned out to be one of them. Sam Bass collected his pay, got drunk, bought a new lariat rope, and tried it out by roping an old man and dragging him along so his face scraped in the gravel of the road. The sheriff was called but Sam had taken off for Texas, and all they ever heard of him was that he was mortally wounded in 1878 while staging a train robbery.

Teddy worked with his father's cattle for the next six years, all the time listening to stories told by the Texas cowboys about their trail-herding experiences. He learned from them and from the Pawnee Indians whom he liked to visit. His attempt to join the tribe so he could hunt buffalo was blocked by the old Chief who told him sternly, "No, your father say we stole you, make plenty trouble for Indians."

He left Nebraska for good in 1878, when his father told him to plow the West Ridge. (Teddy knew that farming was not for him.) He hired on with an outfit taking cattle to the Pine Ridge Indian Agency in South Dakota. He took in the sights of Deadwood, drifted down to Texas, and signed up to go on the trail with a herd of cattle belonging to Print Olive,

"Teddy Blue" Abbott, open range cowboy. *Photo courtesy of Montana Historical Society, Helena.*

who was on trial for murder. His brother, Ira, was sent as trail boss, and he shot one of his Mexican cowboys in an argument over the way the cattle were being handled.

Once in a storm the trail herd stampeded, and the four men assigned to herd them could not stop the milling cattle. In the morning, Teddy realized that one of the four men was missing. They found him and his horse, both trampled to death by the herd. As a result of this and similar incidents, orders went out from all trail bosses that the cowboys were to sing when running with a stampeding herd so their co-workers would know where they were.

Teddy was learning fast how it was in the "Wild West" and that a man was lucky to hang on to his life, let alone his health. Word came later that Print Olive had taken off after two men he accused of rustling and in the fight that followed, his brother, Bob, got killed. The sheriff took the two men, but Print got them away from him and hanged them. Print went to jail for a year or two, got out, and was shot in '86 over a ten-dollar livery bill that a cowboy owed him.

In the spring of 1880, Teddy hired on with the CY outfit. He and four other fellows were to go into Oregon and bring out a herd of cattle, but at Cheyenne they met a cowpuncher who had been on that trail and said he was wet every day for three weeks. The five men decided to head south instead and ended up on the sandy sagebrush flats of Alamosa, Colorado. There Teddy got into a Monte game and won enough money to buy a horse to go with the saddle he already owned.

He was then able to hire on to help drive Bill Charlton's 700 horses into Nebraska for sale to settlers. As they drove these horses, they broke them to ride. On one occasion, Teddy rescued Bill Charlton, whose spur had caught when he was bucked off the horse; Bill later gave the horse to Teddy for saving his life. After they crossed Colorado, Teddy got sick and had to leave the outfit. Mountain fever, they called it.

When he recovered, Teddy and his friends wandered around, finally getting into a fight in a theater—that prompted Teddy to walk hurriedly down an alley and board a train for LaVeta, Colorado, where he picked up his horse. He drifted down to Mexico and worked a fall roundup for John Chisum on the Pecos River. That was such a desolate country, Teddy went to El Paso but he found so much shooting there he decided to take a job with John Blocher, who was trailing a herd to Ogallala, Nebraska.

When he got there, Teddy went to see his family because he had a $3,000 inheritance coming from relatives in England, and he had spotted a ranch in Colorado that he wanted to buy. Teddy was twenty-one then, and his father warned that at the rate he was going, his inheritance money would all be gone before he was twenty-five. Teddy beat the odds; he went to town, got sick, started drinking, spent a lot of money on a girl, and in three years it was all gone.

Teddy got a job repping for the Olive outfit and was assigned to Buffalo Bill Cody's wagon. Cody was foreman of the ranch that sold 500 head of cattle to the Swan Brothers at LaBonte, Wyoming. John Fletcher, Albert Cochran, and Poinsett Barton, who had helped drive a Texas trail herd to Wyoming, needed jobs so they received the herd at Horse Creek and drove them to the Swan Brothers' Ranch. After collecting their pay for the job and encountering some cold weather, they got on a Union Pacific train and went back to Texas.[1]

Teddy and Bill Cody got along very well together, but something always seemed to come up that kept their wagon and outfit from arriving on time. One day, Cody brought out a spring wagon loaded with whiskey; he then started horse races and shooting contests and had the men trying to rope jackrabbits. The cowboys swore that one man actually did rope a rabbit. When Cody's wagon didn't come in with the Olive beef herd to be shipped to market, Cody was fired off the roundup crew.

The next job for Abbott was helping his friend, Bill Paxton, bring a herd up the trial to Miles City in 1884. After Paxton got the herd to Montana, he was hired as boss of the outfit, but he got drunk so many times and did so much gambling that he had to be replaced; after that, no one would hire him even as a plain cowboy.

Teddy was learning more and more about trail herding. The average crew was made up of eleven men: eight cowboys to handle the herd, one horse-wrangler, a cook, and the boss. The least-skilled cowboys worked with the drags as these animals dropped to the rear of the herd.

Buffalo Bill Cody, foreman of the Print Olive Cattle Pool and for some time an open range cowboy. Teddy Blue Abbott worked for Cody and even tried out for his Wild West Show. *Photo courtesy of Buffalo Bill Historical Center, Cody, Wyo.*

The dust there was so bad, it covered the men's faces and got in their mouths and throats; the experienced cowboys wouldn't settle for that job. Going into a new country, the trial boss had to ride ahead to find water so the cowboys could steer the herd toward it. In watering a herd, the pointers headed the lead cattle downstream to get them to clear water first. As the herd and finally the drags kept coming, they could all get clear water as they worked upstream.

The greatest hardship on the trail was lack of sleep. The regular day ended at nine o'clock when the men had gotten the herd bedded down for the night. After that the regular cowboys had to take turns at night-herding in two-hour shifts. At 3:30 a.m. the cook beat on a dishpan and yelled, "Roll out," so if a man had gotten even a few hours sleep, he was lucky. If anyone complained to the boss, he'd say, "What in hell are you kicking about; you can sleep all winter in Montana."[2]

Teddy met a preacher's daughter in Miles City who tried to convert him, but she realized that the attempt had failed when she saw him later with a lady of questionable character. Also in Miles City he went to Turners' Theatre where he met another lady-of-the-night who invited him to her room. As they started out from back-stage, he tripped and fell through a thin partition onto the stage of the theatre. When he realized where he was, he grabbed a chair and, using it as a bucking horse, shouted, "Whoa Blue, whoa Blue," which was a common cowpuncher's expression. Then the manager yelled, "Hey Blue, come out of there" and the audience yelled and laughed. From that time on, he was no longer plain Teddy, but Teddy Blue.

A row with the boss at the FUF over a steer they had killed for beef led to the dismissal of all the cowboys, but they were soon rehired as the outfit needed them, and the boys needed midwinter work. In the spring, Teddy Blue left the FUF for good and went to work for Matt Winters, who was running an outfit for T. J. Bryan on Otter Creek in the Powder River country. Winters sent him to rep with Cap Howe at an outfit higher up on the creek. When the Otter Creek roundup was over, Abbott went to work for the N Bar outfit* owned by the Newman brothers of St. Louis. Zeke Newman, the roundup boss, sent him to rep with outfits bordering the N Bar range. That fall, Teddy quit the beef roundup to go down to the Powder River and meet two N Bar trail herds coming up from Texas. John Burgess was in charge of the first and John Bowen was in charge of the second herd. Ten days later they got to the Yellowstone River and forded it near Fort Keogh. One of their men fell off his horse and was near drowning, but someone yelled to him, "Grab a steer by the tail." He did and the steer pulled him across the river and up the bank.

After they crossed the Yellowstone with the herd, Teddy Blue and Harry Rutter decided to go to Miles City, although they were in the half of the

---

* Later owned by the Joe Watts family.

Swimming cattle across the Yellowstone River, and using a row boat to guide them. *Photo courtesy of the Range Riders Museum, Miles City, Montana.*

crew that was supposed to stay with the trail herd. The next day, Johnny Burgess came to town and fired Teddy, who said, "Give me fifty-cents to cross on the Yellowstone ferry and I'll go get my bed." Burgess gave it to him, and they had a couple of drinks and pretty soon he said,[3] "Hell, I've done a lot worse than that myself, go on back to the herd." After they got the cattle up to the mouth of the Musselshell River, Newman asked Burgess which man he was going to keep on for the winter and he said, "Teddy Blue." Newman asked why he would keep on a new man with the outfit. Burgess said, "Because he can sing," and with that Newman, an owner who was paying the bills, snorted and said, "If you think I'm going to pay $40 a month for a music box for you fellows all winter, you're crazy." Then Burgess said, "That's all right. The night never gets so dark nor the river so deep that Teddy isn't right there with the herd."

The delicate little English boy had grown up to prove his worth even on the most rugged of western frontiers.

The second herd of N Bar cattle came in a few days later. They had struck a snow storm and had to build a string of fires to keep warm. All twenty cowboys from the two drives went to Miles City to celebrate. Fifteen of them got on the next train out and went back to Texas.

Along toward spring, Burgess put Teddy Blue to digging post holes as he wanted to fence a pasture, but when the roundup boss saw that Teddy had only scratched the top soil, he fired him.

Abbott went to work for the D.H.S. as he had heard that Granville Stuart had two good-looking daughters and that he always treated his cowpunchers fair and square. Teddy was also remembering that it was Stuart who led a group of fourteen vigilantes that had hanged or shot seventeen rustlers and put an end to cattle stealing in the area. Abbott found good treatment and wonderful grub at the D.H.S. so he spent most of the winter at the home ranch of the Stuart's and at Reece Anderson's, as there were dances and roller skating parties with the Stuart girls and their friends. He made himself popular by carrying wood and water and wiping dishes for the cook. In the spring, Stuart sent him to rep with the Moccasin outfit. Teddy also worked with the Judith Basin Pool where he met their horse-wrangler, Charlie Russell, and the two became great friends. At this point, Teddy Blue admitted that he had tried to marry a pretty Cheyenne girl, but she wouldn't have him. After the fall beef roundup, the D.H.S. boss sent Abbott to work with the trail herds that were being taken across the Missouri, but by the time they started on the second herd, winter set in and the river froze. The men put dirt on the ice and tried to get the cattle over anyway. Some of them made it. The herds still on the South side of the river scattered and tried to get back to the home range. The winter of '87 and '88 was so severe that by spring most of the cattle on both sides of the river were dead. People said it was that winter that broke the back of the range cattle industry in Montana.

The worst storms set in right after Christmas in '87 and the cattle drifted toward the Missouri. The few cowboys couldn't hold them away and thousands of cattle went down in the airholes in the river ice. Teddy Blue was riding with Pike Landusky* that winter and learned a lot about survival from that tough old pioneer. Pike taught him to make a mask out of the black lining of a coat to avoid snow blindness, but not until Teddy had spent five days in bed with a bad case of it. Pike also showed him how to dress "so if you break your leg and lay out on the prairie you won't freeze to death." The men stayed close to their own camps and at the Landusky cabin in the Little Rockies. During the winter, they had to go to Rocky Point for additional supplies, but while they were on their way, they ran into an Indian camp and stayed there a week having a good time.

The men estimated that the D.H.S. lost six-thousand head of cattle, largely in 1887-88. When they went to round up the cattle in the spring, they found mostly steers and dry cows and a few yearlings. The river and all the coulees were full of dead cattle.

Back at the ranch, Stuart assigned him the job of repping for the D.H.S. and outfitted him with new pants, hat, gun belt, and a six-shooter. Teddy had been to the town of Maiden and blew his $40 paycheck and was broke.

Then he met Mary Stuart again, decided to quit drinking, threw his tobacco away, and stopped even his limited gambling. He also got the chip off his shoulder and stayed out of fights. Teddy was secretly engaged to Mary, although her mother wanted him to marry Katie, the older sister.

While working for the D.H.S., Teddy and Stuart's son, Dick, had a "tenderfoot" riding with them, and it was a job to keep him from getting lost or in trouble. "He wasn't a good hand like Teddy Roosevelt or Oliver Wallop." The last work Abbott did for the D.H.S. was to take some bulls to the Milk River country. He didn't like the new foreman, so he went to work for the Bar 72 on the Moccasin roundup. This outfit forded the Missouri with a herd near Great Falls. Then he gathered horses for the PW, a small cow outfit on the Musselshell, and later repped for them on six different outfits. That fall he left the PW with sixteen horses and twenty-five head of cattle of his own, driving them over the Judith Mountains.

He left the livestock near the Stuart Ranch and went on to see Mary late one night. Soon after that, Mrs. Stuart died of a fever and Katie died of consumption. Six months later, in 1889, Teddy Blue and Mary were married and went to live on a little cattle ranch to which he soon added a homestead. They had five boys and three girls, all of whom had successful lives. In 1939, the Abbotts celebrated their fiftieth wedding anniversary.

Teddy Blue Abbott's cowboy days spanned the '70s and '80s—the years of open range and cattle pools. In all those cow camps, Teddy was known as a great story teller—often stretching the truth, his friends said, and

---

* Later shot by Kid Curry.

Ferrying cowboys across the Yellowstone River. *Photo courtesy of E. J. Cameron, J. H. Trafton, and the Range Riders Museum, Miles City, Montana.*

in the end he wrote a book to preserve for all time those cowboy adventures in the heyday of cattle raising in Montana when herds numbered in the thousands.

"Hell, " said his friend, Kid Amby, when he read the book, "if only a fourth of what he tells is true, it still makes good history."

References:
[1] Fletcher, Baylis John, *Up the Trail in '79* (University of Okla. Press, Norman, 1966), pp. 61-64.
[2] Abbott, E.C. (Teddy Blue) and Helen Huntington Smith, *We Pointed Them North* (University of Okla. Press, Norman, 1966), p. 68.
[3] Ibid.
[4] Fletcher, Baylis John, *Up the Trail in '79* (University of Okla. Press, Norman, 1966).

DOC NELSON, WHO RODE THE BRONC TO BREAKFAST
CHAPTER NINE

Frank "Doc" Nelson was another of the early-day cowboys who worked for the Judith Basin and other cattle pools. He was born in 1867 at Old Central Park in the Gallatin valley of pioneer parents who had settled there in 1864.[1] The Nelson family eventually included seven brothers and a sister. Unlike most of the other cowboys who had "come up the trail" or had wandered in from neighboring states, Nelson was a native-born Montanan. He remembered as a boy going to Virginia City and seeing the Chinese men mining the bedrock of Alder Gulch.[2]

Frank, who was better known as "Doc," got his first riding job when he was fifteen and "hired on" with the RL outfit and then with the Two Dot Wilson spread. The Wilson outfit was managed by Doc's brother, Beaver Nelson. It was located at Living Springs, northeast of the present town of Harlowton. For some time, he wrangled horses there and also met Charlie Russell, who was later to draw Doc in several of his paintings.

He also met a cook known only as Nicholson. The cook had a son, Si, who ran with a questionable partner called California Ed. Under Ed's direction, Si and others of the gang decided to stampede a large bunch of horses and drive them off, presumably heading across the Missouri River and into Canada where they could sell them for a good profit. Doc, Beaver, and several other Two Dot cowboys picked up the trail of the horses that had been stolen from Two Dot and on the second day caught up with the thieves.

Since it was the "law" of the open range that horse thieves were always hanged, there was a shoot-out in which Si and Ed were killed by the foreman, Beaver, and his men while young Doc held the saddled horses. The cowboys laid the two bodies under a cut-bank that they caved off to cover them. They all agreed to tell Nicholson, the cook and father of Si, that the thieves had escaped without being recognized.

Several years later, Doc went to work for the Judith Basin Pool; Russell was also working there. Doc's unscheduled ride into camp one morning

Two Dot Wilson had a big cattle spread that ranged around the town of Two Dot and extended for many miles in every direction. He took Doc Nelson in and even tried to legally adopt him, but that plan didn't work out. *Photo courtesy of the Meagher County Historical Society.*

on a bucking horse was documented by the artist in one of his most famous paintings, "Bronc to Breakfast." The incident was also immortalized by Francis E. White in the "Charles Russell Suite" musical produced in Bozeman in 1963 with the words from one song:[3]

> Hey, Doc, git that bog-spavined hoss outa the stew kettle!
> That Roman-nosed cayuse is just kickin' all the breakfast in
>   the fire.
> I'll take his hide . . . You hear? Doc, do you hear?
> I'll skin him alive while he's still kickin'!
> I'll shoot him so full of holes that his hide won't hold hay!
> Hey, Doc, dad blast yer hide . . . Grab his head Amby.
> Never mind the bacon or Doc; just save the cawfee . . .!
> You got everybody just as mad as . . . . . . Hey!
> We got a bronc to breakfast, shure enuff.

Many years before the musical, Amby Cheney and Doc Nelson had met with Russell in Bozeman and talked about the picture. Russell identified Doc as the man on the horse and Amby as the man on the wheel of the cook wagon. Amby remembered that the cook's name was Fred Graham and that the two men sitting on the ground to his left were part-Indian cowboys but he couldn't remember their names. Russell had painted himself as the sitting cowboy to the right of the bucking horse. Bert Jackson, another open range cowboy, said he was the man standing by the one in white chaps. Bert knew a lot about cowboying and could relate stories of the old days right up to the time he died at age 102. He and Doc had both ridden the "rough string" horses.

It was during the summer of '84 that an event occurred which proved to what length the cowboys would go to get a laugh. On this occasion, Doc was riding on the Judith River below Lewistown with three other cowboys looking for cattle. One of them was Charlie Brewster, who was known for his very dry wit. It was a cold, raw day, so they rode on to a protected south slope above a steep embankment where they could sit in the sun and have a smoke. Below them, growing out from this bank were some scrubby pine trees. As they sat there rolling cigarettes, Charlie said, "Give me a match." Someone handed him a big wooden match. As he struck it on the brass cover of his stirrup, the match flared with a sharp crack startling his horse. As the horse jumped, the bank caved in, letting horse and rider fall into the top of a big pine tree below. Hung up—completely high-centered but with Charlie Brewster still in the saddle. Now, according to the story Russell told around the campfire that evening, Brewster looked up at his pals and said, "Throw me another match; that one went out." Well, those cowboys tossed their ropes down to Charlie and he tied them to his horse and saddle and the boys on top pulled him right out of there. Back in camp, Russell started making sketches and eventually completed a painting which depicted the humorous side of a near-tragic incident. It was one of Doc's regrets that he never saw the finished picture. Doc is also the cowboy riding a bald-faced horse in Russell's painting, "The Herd Quitter."

Nelson had a close call, too, when he was with a "rep" outfit near the fork of the Big Horn and Yellowstone rivers. He had come in tired from riding, so right after supper, he took his saddle for a pillow and lay down to sleep. A big fellow named John Matt, who'd had a little argument with Doc earlier, came riding into camp very drunk. Seeing Doc lying there, Matt let out a curse, pulled out his gun, and shot Doc, grazing the skin behind his ear. Doc said if it had been any closer, it would have gone into his skull and any farther away, it would have taken his ear off.

The other cowboys grabbed Matt, but before they could do anything with him, he passed out. They carried him up the hill a ways and left him there to sleep off his drunk. One of the cowhands told Doc, "You jump Matt in the morning and then I'll take over, because I have been wanting to get him anyway."

"Bronc to Breakfast" by C. M. Russell. "Doc" Nelson on the bucking horse; Kid Amby Cheney on the wagon wheel; Frank Graham is the roundup cook; Russell on the ground at the right; Bert Jackson holding the horse at the left. *Photo courtesy of Montana Historical Society, Helena.*

But early the next morning before anyone was up, Matt came down, awakened Doc, and apologized profusely, begging Doc to forgive him as he said he was so drunk he didn't know what he was doing when he shot him. John Matt left that "rep" outfit as soon as he could get his paycheck. Later, Matt was involved in a shooting over a poker game and was killed. The man who killed him was acquitted and told to just go back to work because it was well known that Matt had tried to kill Doc Nelson.

Doc helped move the big herds of cattle across the Missouri River into the Milk River and Canadian ranges, but he didn't stay to work them there. He came back to the Bozeman area, bought a livery stable, and ran that for about three years. He tried mining for a while—one season at the Wickes Camp near Helena and another at a mine near Ogden, Utah. After that, he returned to Bozeman and spent the rest of his life in that area.

References:
[1] Wolcott, Phyllis, *The Saga of Doc Nelson* (Gallatin Co. Hist. Soc., n.d.), pp. 1-4.
[2] *The Madisonian*, Virginia City, MT, 1959.
[3] *Billings Gazette*, April 28, 1963, p. 9.
[4] *Judith Basin Press*, Stanford, MT, April 9, 1964.

KID CURRY, OUTLAW COWBOY
CHAPTER TEN

K id Curry was one of the more famous, or infamous, cowboys of both the Judith Basin and Bearpaw cattle pools. The notorious Curry brothers were among the most wanted outlaws of northern Montana during the last decade of the nineteenth century, and of all the family, the Kid had the worst reputation.

When the Currys came up the trail from Wyoming soon after the "Rustler's War" there, they seemed to be law-abiding under the leadership of the oldest brother, Henry. This brother, commonly called Hank, settled on a ranch near Landusky, a gold camp in the Little Rockies south of Malta. His brothers, Lonnie, Johnny, and Harvey (better known as "Kid Curry"), either worked with him or found jobs with the large roundups or cattle pools in northern and central Montana. At one time all three of them worked for Robert Coburn and his Circle C outfit. It was rumored that Wallace, Will, and young Bob Coburn were involved in minor escapades with the Currys and the Hole-in-the Wall gang and that two of them possibly had notches in their guns, but they were not directly involved in the shooting of Pike Landusky or in the train robberies.

The Currys, who had for some reason changed their name from Logan to Curry, built up a herd of several hundred horses; they also owned four or five hundred head of cattle. They seemed to be prosperous and well-liked, but with Hank's death the family fell apart and the younger brothers began to run with the "Wild Bunch," which included Butch Cassidy and Harry Longabaugh, better known as the Sundance Kid. Others in that "bunch" were Tod Carver, Ben Kilpatrick, and George Parker.

In the summer of 1890, Kid Curry was working for the Circle O Bar (Stevens outfit) of the Moccasin Pool northeast of Lewistown while his brothers were working for neighboring outfits. However, the Kid was always the wildest one of the Curry gang, and one day when the cowboys of the Judith Basin roundup were camped on Crooked Creek north of the Moccasin Mountains, gathering cattle to be taken across the Missouri River, a big sorrel horse came pitching and bucking down Blood Coulee right past Kid Amby Cheney and into the roundup camp. The man who was riding him "straight up and to the finish" was Kid Curry. When he asked Plunkett, the roundup boss, for a job, he was hired at once. The outfit had a big job to do and there was plenty of work for a cowhand that could ride like that.

Kid Curry, who was about twenty years old then, helped them gather Basin Pool cattle which were stragglers from the many herds that were already across the Missouri and into the new Bearpaw Pool. It was late fall when they got the stragglers across the river, and Kid Amby was sent to rep with the Circle C (Coburn outfit). It was then that Kid Curry also went to work for the Coburns.

The cowboys working for the Judith Basin Pool were busy moving the cattle across the Missouri and into the new Bearpaw Pool to greener pastures in the mountains and along the Milk River. The owners of these herds were big cattlemen who lived in Helena or Butte, like Kaufman and Stadler, Phelps and Pruitt, and Kohrs and Bielenberg. They viewed with alarm the settlement of the Judith Basin by ranchers and sheepmen and the end of an era of open cattle ranges there.

It was estimated that during the springs and summers of 1890 and 1891 over 100,000 head of cattle were moved across the river. When a herd of possibly 2,500 had been gathered, they were pushed into the Missouri River at Clagett near the mouth of the Judith and forced to swim across. The cowboys had to be in and out of the river most of the time. It was dangerous and demanding work that required a man with courage who was also good with a horse. Not every cowboy wanted to work the river crossing, so it was small wonder that men like Kid Curry were hired on with no questions asked.

Even after he quit work with the Bearpaw Pool roundups and the Circle C, the Kid kept out of serious trouble until he had a quarrel with Old Pike Landusky, owner of a saloon in the town that was named for him.

According to Amby Cheney, "Pike was known as a 'mean devil' who always carried a gun. He walked with a gold-headed, weighted cane, and it was said that he often used it on a bystander at the bar whether he was making trouble or not."[1]

Pike's business rival just across the street was "Jew Jake," a one-legged fellow whose missing leg had been shot off in some scrape in Great Falls, Montana. Jew Jake used his rifle as a crutch when he walked and kept it slung around his neck when he sat down. Old-timers said he often sat out on his porch waiting for trouble with Pike.

Amby Cheney is also quoted as saying, "Some say that Kid Curry and Pike got into an argument over a woman; others say it was over a plow that the Currys had borrowed from Pike and returned to him badly broken." Others said[2] that Pike didn't want his step-daughter to have anything to do with handsome but wild Lonnie Curry, with whom she was having secret trysts. So Pike was said to have arranged to have Kid Curry and Lonnie arrested on a trumped-up cattle branding charge. After they were arrested, Pike was made a deputy sheriff, and he took the boys to jail in Fort Benton, put them in chains, and beat them up. Due to lack of evidence, the Kid and Johnny were released, but they never forgot the troubles caused by Pike, and the Kid swore he would kill Pike Landusky or get killed by him.

Later on, the fatal shot was witnessed by many. Kid Curry was standing at the bar in Pike's saloon, and the argument began. During the struggle, Pike, who was hampered by a heavy coat and getting badly beaten, reached for his gun. The gun misfired, but the Kid was quick on the draw, too, and the saloon man was killed instantly. The Kid's "back-up" men had kept Pike's gunmen quiet during the fight.

Kid Curry took to the hills and the sheriff was in Fort Benton, two hundred miles from Landusky. A short time after Pike was killed, a fellow came into the saloon at Landusky and told Kid Amby that someone wanted to see him outside. When he went out, he found Tom Clary, the sheriff. After shaking hands, he asked Amby if he knew where to find Kid Curry. Amby said, "Honest, I don't know where he is." Clary then told Curry's pals that if they saw the Kid to tell him to come in and give himself up. The law officer promised to let him off easy because of Pike's quarrelsome reputation.

Not long after Pike's death, Johnny Curry "sort of throwed in with" Mrs. Landusky. In the meantime, Jim Winters, the roundup cook, claimed to have bought the Landusky Ranch and went to live there. One day, Johnny rode up to the door of the ranch house and ordered Winters off the place, telling him that if he didn't leave by a certain date, he would come back and shoot him with a double-barrelled shotgun. Winters was known as a peaceful man, but when Johnny rode up to the cabin on the appointed day, Winters opened the door and shot him. A short time after this, Winters foolishly went out after dark to the nearby spring for a bucket of water. He was shot and killed, and it was presumed that Kid Curry had come back and killed Winters to avenge Johnny's death.

Johnny and Winters were both dead; the law of the frontier had settled the matter.

Johnny Curry had been in trouble before. He had lost one arm in a fight with a neighbor known only as "the Dutchman." One day when John was driving in his cart from the ranch near Landusky to Rocky Point on the Missouri, he met the Dutchman traveling in a buckboard drawn by two horses. After they had passed each other, they stopped and each turned around and began shooting. The Dutchman must have been the better shot for he hit Johnny in the arm just above the elbow. A bunch of cowboys that came along soon afterwards found Johnny's horse and cart, and they trailed him to where he had crawled to a waterhole in a coulee. He was a terrible sight—covered with blood and dirt, his wounded arm hanging by a few cords. One of the cowboys loped to camp and got the bed-wagon. They loaded Johnny on it and took him to Malta, where they put him on a train and sent him to the hospital in Fort Benton.

1. Ben Kilpatrick, 2. Harry Longabaugh, 3. Wm. Carver, 4. Harvey Logan, and 5. Butch Cassidy. After robbing the bank at Winnemucca, Nevada, the "Wild Bunch" spent a good chunk of their money in Texas for these dress-up outfits and their group picture. *Photo courtesy of the American Heritage Center, University of Wyoming, Laramie.*

After Jim Winters was killed, his nephew came from the East to take over the old Landusky place. This young man, named Gill Winters, was a typical Eastern "dandy" and hardly a match for the Curry gang. One day, he was missing along with his horse and saddle and the cowboys conjectured that the Currys got him.

Little more was heard from the Curry gang for some time. Kid Curry had disappeared, Johnny was dead, and Lonnie had drifted out of the country. A cattle outfit from over toward Big Sandy came to the ranch, rounded up the stock, and drove them off, claiming the Currys owed them money.

Then on July 3, 1902, a Great Northern passenger train was held up at Exeter Creek near Wagner, west of Malta. It was said by authorities to be the work of the Curry gang. One old cowboy, Guy Tullock, who died in Lewistown a number of years ago, said he was riding near the "hold up" and hid in the brush until the Currys rode away. Why didn't he report the incident? Well, if you valued your life in those days, you didn't tangle with the Currys.

Tom Clary, the sheriff, formed a posse of cowboys in the area and went in search of the train robbers. Kid Amby Cheney and his brother, Melve, said that none of the members of the posse were anxious to find the Curry gang. Blood would undoubtedly be shed, and besides that, many of the cowboys in the posse were close friends of the Currys. Actually, the Currys were sort of the Robin Hoods of the Milk River country as they often helped poor ranchers and neighbors, supplying them with horses and cattle with no questions asked about where the stock came from. Some of the other men who rode on this posse with the Cheney brothers were Johnny Griffin, George Barrows, former roundup boss Plunkett, Con Price, Gus Hammer, Bruce Glenn, Tullock, Pete Vann, "Wild Bill" Sutter, Mexican Joe Contlon, and Al Malison. The posse spent more time in bars and stalling around than they did on the trail of the train robbers.

The Currys were never seen in the Milk River country again. Rumors were that both the Kid and Lonnie had gone to their old hide-out in Hole-in-the Wall, Wyoming. They were close friends of Butch Cassidy who had spent a short time in north-central Montana and had been arrested, after escaping from authorities in Kansas City. Another unverified report was that they were all in Argentina, still working as cowboys. But after the robbery, the Currys never returned to their old haunts in the Little Rockies.

The late Sid Willis, a Bearpaw Pool cowboy, who at one time was sheriff of Valley County (then comprising about one-third of eastern Montana), claimed to have been the last man in the country to see Kid Curry. They had both worked for the Bearpaw Pool in earlier years.

Willis was the proprietor of the Old Mint Saloon in Great Falls, which once housed a most famous collection of Russell paintings. He told Kid Amby that one night soon after the Great Northern train hold-up, Kid Curry came to the back door of the Mint. Willis let him in and the Kid said, "I'm in real trouble this time. For God's sake get me some money if you can. I've got to get out of the country." Willis said he told Curry that he would give him the money and asked him to wait while he got it from the safe, which was upstairs. Before he left the room, Willis noticed that Curry was carrying a small suitcase. When Willis came back a few minutes later, Kid Curry and the suitcase were gone. "I guess he thought I'd gone to notify the sheriff," Willis said. "He didn't trust me, but I was coming with the money because I knew what he would get and what I might get if I turned him in."

Perhaps the loot from the train robbery was in that bag; we will never know. Kid Curry was never again seen in Montana.

References:
[1] Cheney, Elizabeth McGiffin (as told to her by Kid Amby Cheney), "Kid Curry and his Brothers," *True West*, March-April 1962, pp. 68-70.
[2] Cheney, Roberta C., *Names on the Face of Montana* (Mountain Press, Inc., Missoula, MT, 1984), pp. 160-161.
[3] Coburn, Walt, *Pioneer Cattleman of Montana, The Story of the Circle C Outfit* (Univ. of Okla. Press, Norman, 1968).

WALTER JACKSON, MONTANA'S FIRST BLACK COWBOY
CHAPTER ELEVEN

Many black cowboys came from Texas to Montana with the trail herds, but they returned to the South as soon as the cattle were delivered and the wages collected. . .all except George Jackson. He came early in the 1880s and hired on with the Quarter Circle U Ranch. His job was to break wild horses, a dangerous occupation that he survived—only to be killed in a fall from a log bridge that he was helping build across a canyon.

That was shortly before the birth of his son, Walter, who was the first black baby to be born in Montana. Walter's mother had come north with her father, George Shelton, who had been raised by a Quaker family in Oklahoma. She and the baby boy continued to live on the ranch in a small house provided for them by the ranch owner, George Willison. White cattle owners were establishing ranches and Indians still roamed from one choice hunting ground to another, but a black family was a rarity.

Walter was destined to be a cowboy who worked during the latter part of the open range area. After that he worked for cattle outfits and ranchers who had managed to get control of enough land to support their fairly large herds.

The older cowboys on the Quarter Circle U Ranch adopted Walter as a kind of mascot. "Always called me 'the Kid'," recalled Walter in an interview many years later in his Sheridan, Wyoming, home.[1]

"When I was little, they let me sit on the corral fence to watch them rope the horses and work with the cattle." Wild horses were rounded up and brought in from the Missouri Breaks and from the Pryor Mountains. Walter grew up around the corrals and learned to handle horses, so he naturally fell into the job of taming them.

Walter's mother died when he was thirteen, so from then on, he was on his own. He was already knowledgeable about horses and knew that he wanted, most of all, to work with them. He learned to corral wild horses and finally to break them to ride. Rounding up cattle from the vast open range grazing areas required a lot of saddle horses, and it became Walter's job on the Quarter Circle U Ranch to get horses ready for the other cowboys to use.

Horses for freight teams were also in great demand, as all supplies had to be brought by wagons from the Missouri River boat dock at Fort Benton, or if the river was low, from Clagett. Ten, twelve, or even fourteen horses were required for each jerk-line outfit, and these, too, came from the wild herds.

"Every man that is a good rider isn't a good horse breaker," Walter explained. "It takes a certain kind of 'know-how.' When you break a horse, you break him so anyone can ride him. If he bucks, you want to ride it out of him. Even horses that are broke lose their head sometimes and start bucking. Then you usually have to break them again."

From the time that Walter was old enough to handle a horse until he left Montana, he broke the range mustangs into useable cattle horses and freight teams. The pay for breaking a horse to ride was usually $10. It took longer to convince a wild horse that he should submit to a harness and then pull a wagon along with several other horses. To break a horse for freighting, the charge was $30. Sometimes ranchers would ask Walter to break a horse for packing or for roping and that, too, took more time and brought in a little more money.

Each spring, the ranchers found that some of their saddle horses had left the winter pasture and gone back to the wild bunch. Walter often earned $5 or $10 per head as he and another cowboy retrieved them. To do this, they built a "blind" corral—one completely camouflaged by upright pine trees cut and leaned against the fence. Knowing that wild horses, when pursued, naturally head for the forested ridges, the men were able to herd them into the pine tree corral. The domestic horses reacted calmly to the corral, but the wild ones turned and fought to get out. Some grabbed at the pine poles and left their teeth marks. It was Walter's job to open the gate for the mustangs—while managing to keep out of the way of flying hooves—and to close the gate after them so that the once-tamed animals could be roped in the corral and led back to the ranch.

Jackson recalled that, while he was working in the Smith River Country (south of Great Falls), he left White Sulphur Springs one winter afternoon heading for Three Forks. He was following the Old Dorsey Trail along the foothills of the Flatiron Mountains. The Moss Agate River was on the east side. A ground blizzard came up when he was about halfway to Dorsey. He had planned to stay at the Big Madison Ranch for the night, but he lost his bearings and didn't know where he was. With the weight of a man on his back his horse was floundering in the snowdrifts, so Walter got off. He took his rope and made two half-hitches around the saddle horn and then held onto the other end. The horse was then able to work his way through the drifts and as Walter tightened the rope at intervals, the horse would pull him through, too. Finally, the horse found the ranch gate and as Walter opened it, a bell rang. The cowboys from the Big

Walter Jackson and his No. 1 horse for roping, cutting or trailing.

Madison Ranch came running and asked how he had gotten there at this time of day. Walter explained that he had been on the trail all night. They took his horse to the barn and Walter to the house, but they wouldn't let him near the stove until they had examined his feet and hands to be sure he wasn't frozen. It was 48 degrees below zero, but Walter was O.K.

Old Dorsey* was the great shipping point for the stockmen out of the Smith River Valley. Cattle came in from the open ranges all over that country. There was a flat-bottomed draw just outside of Old Dorsey at the foot of the ridge. There were tent teepees, freight wagons, and roundup wagons until it looked like a village, according to Jackson's account. During shipping time, as many as a hundred people were camped there. By then the Great Northern had built a branch line from Helena to Great Falls, and it ran through the Smith River country.

A lot of cowboys came into Dorsey and some of them would stay at the little hotel. One night, a character named Bill Murray was sitting on the benches in the lobby with the others. The big wood-burning stove that heated the lobby had an iron shaker to be used when the fire needed stirring up. On this particular evening the room was cooling off, so the hotel owner said, "Bill, will you shake down the stove? It's getting cold in here." Bill never smiled, and he didn't answer, but he got up and you could see his white teeth through a big black mustache. He stepped back

* Largely moved to Ringling.

so that he was about ten feet from the stove. He took out his "45" and shot into the stove until he emptied his gun. That shook the fire down and cleared all the cowboys off the benches.

"I knew Charlie Russell from the time I was a boy until I left Montana," Walter said later in the interview. "He was around Great Falls then, and guiding hunters. He had been a night-hawk and then a wrangler for the Basin and Bearpaw cattle pools. He painted a picture called 'The Trappers Last Stand.' He told me about the last time the trappers came out of the mountains in the spring with their furs. The Indians were waiting at the foothills of the mainrange of the Rockies. When the trappers came near, the Indians opened fire on them. The trappers lay behind their horses to shoot back at the Indians. Charlie said he thought it would make a good picture. It did, too, and it hung in the Conrad Bank on Central Avenue until some New Yorkers came and bought it.

"I knew Brother Van, too, and one time Charlie Russell painted a picture of him riding along a buffalo herd helping the Indians get their winter meat. The trail went down what is now Main Street of Great Falls."

Walter said he heard Brother Van several times; he would preach awhile and then sing awhile. At first the cowboys said, "Brother Van has lost his mind" because none of the other preachers that came around would mix with the cowboys and Indians, but they finally got used to Brother Van and showed up when a service was announced for Utica or Fort Benton.

The last time Walter saw circuit rider Van Orsdel was in 1909. A townsite company was starting up a town about 40 miles out of Conrad. Brother Van showed up, as usual, to establish a church. He was there on the grounds when they had a big drawing for lots in the proposed town of Valier. He was with some other fellows when they rode into the grounds. "He pointed to me and said, 'See that lad over there? He's a Montana boy.' It was a hot September day but I had my sheepskin coat rolled up and tied on the cantle of the saddle. Brother Van went on, 'See that sheepskin? That shows he's a Montana boy.' "

Walter saw the first piece of lumber come on the grounds to build the town of Valier. A short-line narrow-gauge railroad had been laid out from Conrad to bring in supplies. All they had on the grounds that day was a tarpaper hotel one hundred feet long. Chartered passenger cars brought in possible investors from St. Louis, Kansas City, Omaha, and Chicago. These people had no idea what they were coming to. Until a few days before, it had been open range with nothing but cow camps and horses.

Wearing finery with diamond necklaces and rings, the visitors slept in double-decker bunks in that tarpaper "hotel." Guards were put out at night for their safety. Walter worked as a guard for several nights. It was quite a sight for the cowboys who gathered around from time to time to see the dressed up Easterners who had come to buy land.

Walter told of another friend. "Some folks didn't much approve of him and said I'd get into trouble if I stuck around Indian Joe. He was a half-breed and for four years was Chief of Police on the Flathead Reservation. He was college educated, too, at Carlisle Indian school. Joe was always good to me but I sort of guessed that outlaw blood ran in his veins. People said he was one of the smartest outlaws and that he got away with more than most of them did. He would plan big hold-ups and carry them out. He was a big-time gambler, always wore white or light gray shirts, but never had the top button fastened. Instead he tied a blood-red silk handkerchief around his neck and tucked it down inside his shirt. He wore a black hat. Indian Joe hung out mostly around Butte, Red Lodge, and Dillon, always staying close to the mountains.

"I was a young fellow, just learning to ride during the time Joe was around. He was a good horseman and taught me a lot. He knew I had a lot of nerve but Joe chose horses for me that weren't too tough so I wouldn't get discouraged."

It was an interesting relationship, the tough half-breed outlaw, protective and gentle, with a young black boy in a pioneer country dominated by full-blood Indians and white men.

"He never called me anything but 'Kid.' Joe would say 'Kid, do you think you can ride that horse? He's pretty tough.' I'd tell him I could, so he would ear the horse down and holler, 'Crawl in the middle of him, Kid,' and turn the horse loose, so it was either ride or get throwed."

Sometimes Indian Joe asked Walter for money, but he always paid it back. "The sheriff jumped me a lot of times and said, 'That Indian is going to get you in trouble. He is a bad man. He may get mad at you and kill you.' I knew Joe would never hurt me and he never did."

One killing that Joe did, he got away with by claiming self-defense. It was on the outskirts of town, where some people were running a store. Joe came one night when they were counting money. When he appeared at the door, they grabbed their guns from the counter. Joe killed both of them.

All the time in those early days when Walter was with Joe, he never asked the boy to go out with him on a hold-up. Years later when they happened to meet in Butte, Joe did ask him to go out with him. Walter noticed a bunch of guys around; they would scatter out and go to different saloons. Walter knew they were outlaws. Most of them wore California pants with buckskin tacked over the knees. Joe met Walter and said, "Kid, do you want to go out with me tonight? We're going to have some fun." But Walter knew better than to go. That turned out to be the night of one of the biggest hold-ups in Butte. Dave Charles' saloon was all lit up, and there was all kinds of gambling going on. It was one of the biggest places in the West. They would have gold stacked in piles of $2.50, $5, $10, and $20. One game was Spanish Maudie. When you won, they would reach in the barrel for the gold to pay off. They played roulette, Twenty-one, and all kinds of poker. They had a restaurant, too.

The night of this hold-up, the outlaws went into the gambling room and made all the men who were running the games line up against the wall. The dealers kept 45s on their tables, but the outlaws collected all the guns. They gathered up the money—gold and paper—and loaded it into their saddle bags. They had so much, they just left the silver. They also left all the gamblers' guns in the alley after removing the shells. There was a big stir in Butte the next morning. The law men practically knew that Joe had done it, but they couldn't prove it. All Joe's helpers got a big rake-off from that job.

Joe made his last haul holding up a train out of Red Lodge. He had it well planned but somebody got on the inside and tipped off the railroad man that Joe and his gang were going to hold up the train. While the gang held the engineer, Joe slipped in and got the money; he knew where it was. But the law men were laying for him and shot him down as he was making a run for his horse.

"Most people remember him only as an outlaw," Walter concluded, "But he was a good friend to me. I knew that tough cowboys on the street used to look at me and say, 'Don't bother that kid; Indian Joe will kill anyone who bothers him.' "

Walter knew Dan McKay who ran the 76 wagon out of Miles City for years. Dan was a good cowhand but a little reckless at times. When he had a few drinks, he was kind of overbearing. One time he met a gun-slinger in a Miles City bar, and it seems Dan stroked that Texan's hair the wrong way. They kept drinking and arguing until they both reached for their guns. The Texan won the draw and shot Dan down. Walter watched the whole thing and years later when he met up with that Texan, he gave the man a wide berth.

For several years, Walter broke horses for the cattlemen and sometimes rode circle for them during the spring and fall roundups. He had a good horse of his own and traveled freely about Montana, stopping when he found a rancher in need of a horse-breaker.

Walter drifted over into the Wyoming country and got a job working horses for the Lazy B outfit near Gillette. He knew Tom Tate, Buck Taylor, and Tom Wilson, who had been Buffalo Bill cowboys, and Bunk Hanes, another black cowhand who had come up from Texas with the T Bar 7 outfit. Walter helped gather the horses for the Lazy B outfit when they sold out. Lu Barlow, who had owned the Lazy B, sold it to Billy Bishop over on the Belle Fourche River. Lee Haynes, Little Bones and Big Bones Alderson, Eddie Vines, and Lee Gates were also in that outfit. They all agreed that was the wildest bunch of horses they had ever tried to handle.

Jackson worked on the Bar Eleven during one winter. The ranch was owned by the three Fitch Brothers and their dad, and they ran both cattle and horses. That winter a bunch of their horses gathered during a storm along the side of a long ridge. A heavy storm drifted snow over the ridge, completely covering the horses, and they weren't found until spring. There were twenty-six or twenty-seven head of horses, all standing single file back of the ridge. As the snow melted in the spring, the first thing that the cowboys saw was the tops of the horses' heads with their ears sticking

Walter Jackson in 1973 as he appeared for the T.V. historical production filmed just before his death.

up. With more melting, the men could see the full bodies of the horses, all in a line; they had eaten each others' tails off right up to the backbone. The remains were frozen hard as bullets.

The Keeline outfit was one of the biggest in Wyoming. It was fifty miles south of Gillette in Thunder Basin. Jackson repped for them for four years. "Best cow outfit I ever worked for," he often said. When he left, Mr. Keeline gave him one of the solid copper running irons. These running irons were used to brand calves that were found on the range and had been missed during the regular branding season.

Jackson was a rep for the Double Deuce outfit, too. Their brand was 2_2, and they had a Milliron brand, too. The men were cleaning out all those cattle, getting ready to turn the herd over to the Laurel Leaf company. They were shipping 18,000 head of cattle to Clayton, New Mexico, to winter. Some of them were eight- and nine-year-old steers. There were 40 train loads of cattle and the cowboys who went with them lost only three animals on the trip even though the train got held up in Denver because of washed-out bridges.

"There weren't many colored people around Wyoming then" (Walter always said "colored") but he got acquainted with the chef of a Burlington Northern train and his wife, who ran a boarding house in Gillette. She gave Walter the name and address of her sister in New Jersey, and they corresponded for about a year. All the time, the other cowboys were daring him to go back East and meet this girl, so finally Walter dressed up in his best cowboy boots and Stetson hat and took the train for New Jersey.

He was quite a novelty there. People had romantic ideas about the Wild West and no one there had ever seen a genuine cowboy. Walter had to make up his mind in a hurry because he had to get back to Wyoming in time for the fall roundup. So he asked the girl to marry him and she accepted. They didn't have time to fall in love before they were married, but they did that afterward and had many happy years together. They didn't have any children of their own but they raised three of Helen's sister's children and then one grandnephew.

For the next six years, they lived on the Wyoming ranches where he worked, but Helen was a city girl and never did really like ranch life. They moved to Sheridan, Wyoming, and he worked for the railroad until he retired in 1957.

Helen died and Walter lived alone in a neat little white house in Sheridan. Among his treasures were pictures of his cowboy days, the running iron from the Keeline ranch, and an article from a special issue of the *Casper Star Tribune* that says in part, "One of the few negroes to ever come to the Gillette area was Walter Jackson, an early-day cowboy who worked for Chuck Fitch, John Hines, and the Keelines. He was highly respected by all his friends."

After some twenty years of quiet obscurity, this interview and articles about him in the *Billings Gazette*[2] and the *True West*[3] magazine brought him letters, phone calls, and recognition. The "Black Studies" program at Washington State University in Pullman, Washington, arranged trips and interviews. A television special about him was filmed in Virginia City, but Walter died just the week before it was released. He had enjoyed that year of publicity,[4] and in the middle of it, he said to the author of the articles, "Mrs. Cheney, you done pulled me right out of the bog."

References:
[1] Series of interviews - Roberta Cheney with Walter Jackson.
[2] Cheney, Roberta C. "Cowboys, Killers, and the 'Kid'," *Billings Gazette*, October 21, 1973.
[3] Cheney, Roberta C., "Great Falls' First Black Cowboy," *True West*, March-April 1975.
[4] Cheney, Roberta C., "He Grew Up with the West," *Sheridan* (Wyo.) *Press*, October 27, 1973.

TIMBERLINE AND THE ROAN [1]
CHAPTER TWELVE

This long-geared Texas cowpuncher came up the Chisholm Trail in the early 1880s when there was a heavy movement of cattle into Montana. He went to work for the C.A. outfit of Cruse and Anceney* in eastern Montana. This was the era when cattle outfits like the Circle C, the Circle Diamond, the FUF of the Powder River, the N-N, and the H + were setting up line camps and ranch headquarters in eastern Montana along the Powder and Musselshell rivers. They needed cowboys and hired them on with no questions asked.

Timberline and his friend Dick Randall repped for the C.A. outfit, riding through the herds of those other outfits and bringing back C.A. cattle that had strayed onto other ranges and mixed with those herds.

The other C.A. cowboys knew there was something in Timberline's earlier life that he was trying to get away from, but they never dared ask. Possibly it was the fence-cutting war in Texas, when there had been a lot of killings. He was a real cowhand; the men used to say that Timber could guess what an old cow was thinking before she even thought of it. He was one of the top hands with a trail herd. He talked about riding point and swing in a way that indicated he knew plenty about handling trail herds. He told of pointing the leaders downstream as they came to water, so those that came later would have clear water, too.

Timberline was never far away from one of his long barreled six-guns. Most of the time, he kept one tied down to each leg. He was a "lone wolf," shrewd but unfriendly, and he would never bed down near any of the other cowpunchers.

As reps for the C.A. Cattle Company, Timberline and Dick Randall came in contact with reps and cowboys from outfits like the Circle C, the Circle Diamond, D.H.S. (Malta branch), the Bearpaw Pool, the FUF of the Powder

---

* Forerunner of the "Flying D" Ranch, now owned by Ted Turner. It is near Bozeman and was first put together by Childs and Anceney.

River, the N-N, the H +, and the Long S ranging east of Mosby. There were also the RL outfit on the Musselshell River and the 7D outfit of western South Dakota.

One winter, Dick Randall and Timber were riding from a line camp for the Cruse-Anceney outfit, and they lived in a log cabin with a dirt roof and a dirt floor. There was one window with eight small panes. Often during the winter, Timber would rare up out of his blankets, grab one of his guns, and then go back to sleep. After one heavy snowstorm, the weather turned warm, but the nights were marked with freezing temperatures. Water dripped from the roof of the cabin to form long icicles under the eves. Timber and Dick had just finished supper by candlelight when there was a loud crash outside the cabin. Quicker than a flash, Timber swept the lighted candle off the table with his left hand and two shots from his long barreled gun broke out two panes from the window. Dick tried to reason with him and tell him that the cause of the noise outside was a large icicle that had fallen from the edge of the roof, but Timber was not satisfied until Dick went out and looked for tracks. Dick could never get Timber to tell him his troubles, only that he was wanted in Texas.

Spring came early and Dick and Timber were back at the home ranch getting ready for the spring roundup. The bosses of the C.A. outfit had shipped in a carload of unbroken horses from Oregon, and the cowhands were busy "breaking them out." Timber and Dick, as part of their riding assignment, had to keep an eye on the new horses and see that they didn't start back to Oregon. Horses will, in the spring, try to return to the range where they were born, even if they had been shipped by rail.

Timber had been admiring a big roan horse that was in the bunch and remarked, "I hope I get that roan to break out. I'll make the best cow horse in the spread out of him." There weren't any other hands who wanted to tackle the roan. It was plain to see that he was a good horse, but that the man who broke him to ride would sure earn his money.

Timber got on the roan and sat there taking the bucks, jerks, and twists—and liking them. This convinced Dick that his friend was not only a top cowhand but a "bronc stomper" as well. Before the spring calf roundup was over, the roan proved he had the best cow horse "savvy" of any animal on the spread. By the time of the fall beef roundup of steers and dry cows, Timber had trained the roan to be a top roping and cutting horse, too.

After the beef cattle were rounded up and shipped off to market, the outfit pulled into the home ranch in a heavy rainstorm. The cowboys grabbed their bed-rolls from the mess wagon and made a run for the bunkhouse. . .all except Timber. He chose a hay rake that stood near the bunkhouse. The teeth of the rake were elevated in the air, and Timber threw his tarpaulin over them and made his bed under the tarp. The boys in the bunkhouse were soon sound asleep; it had been a hard day's ride back to the home ranch after getting the beef cattle into the railroad cars.

Dick Randall was a charter member of The Dude Ranchers' Association which was formed in 1926 at Bozeman, Montana.

It was midnight when the C.A. cowboys were wakened by gun shots; they rolled out of their bunks, guns in hands, ready for a shoot-out. They heard more pistol shots and howling. The boss approached the rake, pulled off the tarp, and found Timber with his head jammed between two rake teeth and a smoking gun in each hand. Timber had jumped up in his sleep, got his head stuck between the rake teeth, panicked, and then started shooting. Things quieted down and the cowboys went back to bed, but they all realized that Timber had plenty of trouble on his mind. He knew he could never live it down with the boys of the C.A. outfit.

The next morning, he told the foreman that he wanted his time and the roan horse if the outfit would sell it to him. "The roan is yours," said the foreman. "You've been a good hand and I hate to lose you. Come in the house and I'll give you a bill of sale for the horse and your paycheck."

Timberline rode off in the direction of Wyoming. Dick Randall later heard that Timberline had been working for a cattle outfit in that state. One stormy night he was night-herding, trying to hold the beef herd together in the wind, rain, and lightning. Whether Timber's horse had stumbled or stepped in a badger hole was never known, but he was found lying on the ground with a broken neck, his roan horse standing close by with bridle reins trailing.

Dick Randall went on to start the O.T.O., the first dude ranch in Montana, and was host to the great and the near-great who came from Eastern cities and from foreign countries to get a taste of Western life. Years later, he wrote in longhand this story of his friend.

(Author's note: This manuscript was included in material sent to me when I was asked to write the story of the O.T.O., the Randalls' Dude Ranch: Roberta C. Cheney, Music, Saddles, and Flapjacks, Mountain Press Pub. Co., Missoula, MT 1978.)

References:
[1] Randall, Dick, "The Last of Timberline" (Unpublished manuscript that has been herein revised. Events in '80s and '90s written about 1920).

L ONG GEORGE FRANCIS, SANTA CLAUS OF THE HIGHLINE
CHAPTER THIRTEEN

O ne of the legendary figures in northern Montana was cowboy Long George Francis, who came to be remembered as "the Santa Claus of the Highline." Montana people refer to the mainline of the Great Northern Railroad and the area bordering it as the "Highline." The railroad was built by the late Jim Hill across northern Montana and into Havre in 1887. It was later extended westward after the discovery of Maria's Pass in the Montana Rockies and Steven's Pass in the Cascades.

Little is known of Long George's early life before he showed up on the Highline. He did say that he was born in Idaho and spent his childhood with his father, who was a rancher and trapper on the Shoshone River. He often told that he learned to ride a horse when he was six and felt more at home in the saddle than any place else. To this early training, he probably owed his fame and skill as a rider and roper—"one of the best in the United States," according to the *Havre Plaindealer* newspaper of September 30,1918.

At the age of sixteen, Long George, who by this time had stretched out to a height of six feet, six inches, helped drive a herd of cattle into the country near the Bearpaw Mountains in northern Montana. After working as a cowboy for the Bearpaw Pool and other outfits along the Milk and Missouri rivers, he decided to locate near Havre and build up a cattle ranch of his own.

As a rancher he became a prominent citizen and at one time was constable of the town of Havre. He also became a world champion rodeo rider and roper and head of the Havre Rodeo Association. George rode a beautiful saddle horse named Tony. When he roped a calf at a rodeo exhibition, Tony would back up and hold the rope tight until the calf was safely tied. Then Tony, as well as Long George, would turn toward the grandstand and bow to the applauding audience.

But, sad to relate, there were two sides to this handsome cowboy's character and career. He was also secretly involved with a gang of men

Long George Francis, "Santa Claus of the Highline" on his favorite horse, Tony. *Photo courtesy of H. Earl Clack Museum, Havre, Montana.*

who ran liquor across the nearby Canadian border. Then, too, Long George began to build up his own herd by stealing unbranded calves, not only from his neighbors but also from Canadians. It was rumored along the Highline that he actually stole back some of the calves that he had sold to nearby ranchers before the buyers had time to brand them. A fellow in Sheridan, Wyoming, said that his dad had been involved in some of

Long George's escapades and that in one of them, his father was shot and killed.

George's eventual downfall came, however, from his love of horses and his fondness for fancy dress. As one old cowboy put it, "Long George was the best-dressed cowboy on Milk River." He traded a stolen saddle horse, along with three legally owned ones, to a Havre dealer, E. C. Carruth, for a fancy Alaskan beaver coat. The owner of the horse, Phil Clack of Havre, came along one day and recognized his horse in Carruth's corral. Long George, dressed in his fine beaver coat, was apprehended on the street and arrested immediately. Branding mavericks could be tolerated, but horse stealing ranked right up there with murder.

Long George thought that because of his standing in the community of Havre and his popularity in the country, he would be cleared of the charges. But the jury convicted him, and he left town before the sentence could be pronounced. Francis lived as a fugitive from justice for the next year with a $1,000 reward offered for his capture. He hid out in the Missouri breaks, but after a full year of evading the law, he decided to come into Havre and give himself up. He rode his horse into town, down the Main Street, and up to the Courthouse door.

Long George demanded a retrial, and in a courtroom packed with spectators, he was sentenced to "six to ten years" in the State Penitentiary at Deer Lodge. Francis stood up and secured the judge's permission to speak. "Judge, I've always been a man of my word, and I need a few days to go see my girl before I begin serving my sentence."

Possibly because the defendant had voluntarily given himself up or maybe because it was almost Christmas time, the judge granted the tall cowboy's request.

The day before Christmas in 1920, Long George borrowed a car, loaded it with Christmas gifts, apples, and candy and started out for the lonely little country schoolhouse where his sweetheart taught. It was somewhere north of Havre and near the Canadian border.

A howling Northern blizzard came up suddenly, covering the trail and landmarks. After battling the driving snow for many miles over the now trackless prairie, George lost his way and the car skidded over a steep cut bank onto the thick ice of the Milk River. He was pinned beneath the wreck but managed to release himself only to find that his leg was broken.

When George failed to return at the appointed time, the Hill County sheriff with a posse started out to look for him. They tracked him to the wrecked car and with the bits of evidence reconstructed the story of his trip, of the wreck, of his struggle to free himself from the overturned car, and of the tragedy of the broken leg that made it impossible for him to walk to safety. A few burned matches and some charred seat cushions were mute testimony of the injured man's attempt—and failure—to build a fire and keep himself from freezing to death.

The posse picked up a faint trail in the snow and this led them to

George's lifeless body about three miles from the wrecked car. He had made a rude splint for his leg from an apple crate and had attempted to crawl to the schoolhouse. But when the sheriff's men found him, his slashed throat and a pocketknife in the snow told the story of the final decision of a man who preferred to die by his own hand rather than wait for a slow death by freezing.

It is said that on the day of Long George Francis' funeral in Havre, his faithful horse, Tony, with an empty saddle followed the casket in the funeral procession to the cemetery. After one of the largest funerals ever held in the town, the long lean body of George Francis was laid to rest in the cemetery on a hill overlooking Havre.

Legend has it that the "schoolmarm" sweetheart from the little rural school remained faithful to the memory of Long George, who died in a blizzard trying to bring Christmas treats to her and the children. She never married, but she did become a well known Montana educator, and George's Santa Claus trip became a part of the rich heritage of Montana's history.

References:
[1] Cheney, Elizabeth McGiffin, "Long George Francis," *Great Falls Tribune*, Sunday edition, Great Falls, MT, c. 1957.

MORE COWBOYS OF THE OPEN RANGE
CHAPTER FOURTEEN

With thirty or forty cowboys on a crew, there must have been a myriad of interesting stories—where the men came from and why they ended up in Montana. Most of the stories will go forever unwritten, but here are a few of them.

Charlie Carthrae and his brother, Ad, had come from Missouri to work as Montana cowboys. They got jobs with different outfits and their paths seldom crossed. Back home they had both fallen in love with the same girl, but neither won her hand. As a result of their quarrel over the girl, both headed West to assuage their sorrows by becoming cowboys. Charlie worked for the Judith Basin Pool and became a top rough-string rider. He rode with his stirrups tied to the cinch on either side of the horse as the men often did when they were riding tough, unbroken horses. Tied stirrups gave the rider an advantage when man-handling the broncs. Charlie later married Amby's half-sister, Lena Berges, and took up a homestead in the Judith Basin.

Ad imbibed more freely than Charlie and one time when he stayed too long at the Raynesford Bar, he got into a fight with Pete Vann. Since Pete was getting the best of him, Ad pulled out a knife and disembowled his adversary. Pete grabbed his exposed innards and shouted, "Take me to a doctor." Amby and some other cowboys got him to the doctor who sewed him up. Pete lived to finish his cowboying days, get married, and become a prominent rancher.

Years before this, Charlie Russell had made Pete Vann somewhat famous in his story about how Louse Creek was named: one winter when Pete was riding the grub line—visiting ranches and cow camps in order to stay healthy—he acquired body lice. They were biting and making his life miserable, so he stopped at a bouldered creek, took off his shirt, and laid it on a big rock. He picked up another rock and with that pounded his shirt until he was satisfied that he had gotten even with the little varmints and killed every one. "That," said Russell, "is how Louse Creek got its name."[1]

Well, all the time the Carthraes were working for the pools, they never had anything to do with each other. Twenty years later, they happened to pass on a trail. Both had a string of horses. Ad said, "Hello Charlie," and his brother said, "Hello, Ad," and they rode on without further conversation though they hadn't seen each other for many years.

Then there was Billy Wood. Amby was moving a string of horses from one Judith Basin Pool outfit to another when he met Billy Wood, another Basin Pool cowboy with his string, and they traded several horses. Billy wouldn't linger to visit, seemed in a hurry to get on, and Amby saw him heading for the stage road above Old Stanford. A few hours later, the cowboys found Billy where he had hanged himself on the ridge-pole of a cabin with a brand new rope. They figured that the sheriff, Joe Hammond, must have given Billy that rope as his friends knew that all he had was a very old rope. No one ever found out just what kind of trouble had led Billy to hang himself—maybe financial trouble or some horse stealing or his involvement in illegal cattle branding. The cowboys could only speculate and the sheriff would never say.

Finch David was one of the "characters" in the Judith Basin Pool. He had a high voice and a low one, so he entertained the cowboys by playing tricks on the newcomers, the crew, or visiting reps from other outfits. He could impersonate a man and a woman having an interesting conversation. More than one cowboy went exploring to find "the couple" as the old hands chuckled. Later, Finch was looking around the old Indian graves in trees along the Missouri. He took a pillow from under one dead Indian's head and brought it back to camp. Plunkett, the roundup boss, yelled, "Throw that away—those Indians died in a small-pox epidemic." Most of the cowboys had heard of the small-pox that had killed almost the whole Gros Ventre tribe as they camped near the mouth of the Judith River. The cowboys had to ride a long way downwind along the river to avoid the stench of decaying bodies. The medicine man of the tribe had tried desperately to drive out the "evil spirits" by cutting holes in the ice and plunging the sick Indians into the cold water. The first ones to die were put on platforms high in the trees, but toward the end, there was no one able to give the dead proper rites.

Finch David's daughter married P. W. Korrell, and it was at the Korrell Ranch near Utica that Charlie Russell spent his first night in the Judith Basin. That was in 1881, and during the evening he sketched and painted two pictures on the cover pages of a Mother Goose book. One of the pictures was of the first Indian he had seen. Both pictures hung on spikes in the Korrell bunkhouse for many years. Mrs. Korrell finally rescued them and put them in frames.*

John McGiffin came from Iowa with his two brothers and their families in an emigrant car to Corinne, Utah. They unloaded a team of horses,

---

* The picture is now in possession of their daughter, Barbara, in California.

a covered wagon, a cow, a few farm implements, and all their worldly household goods. It took them sixty days to come overland to the Stockett-Sand Coulee-Giffin area where Nat and Abner settled down, raised stock, founded the coal mines, and finally moved to Great Falls so their children could go to school.

John never did get married or settle down. He spent most of his life in Montana as a rough, tough cowboy. He did a lot of drinking and fighting, but he did visit his brothers occasionally. John's usual appearance at the McGiffin ranch, after one of his drinking bouts, included spurring his bucking horse from head to tail, whooping and hollering, and shooting off his pistol. After finally getting thrown "sky high" from his horse, he would limp into the Nat McGiffin cabin and go to sleep. Apparently he was a full-time cowboy for many years on the Chestnut Valley Roundup, which ranged cattle near the present towns of Cascade and Ulm.

There was a fordable place in the Missouri River just below the railroad bridge. Nat and Abner could take their buggy across there and John often swam his horse across at the ripple when there was low water. The ford is now covered by the water backing up from the Rainbow Falls Dam.

In between his cowboying jobs, John helped his brothers and a brother-in-law, Will Junkin, bring 250 head of cattle, which they had shipped from Iowa to Ogden, Utah, on the long drive to the Stockett-Sand Coulee-Giffin area. Throughout his life, John evaded ranch work as much as possible, and for long periods of time the family would have no idea where he was; no one seemed to know when or where he disappeared from the Great Falls area. He was seldom discussed in the family circles. A nephew, Bud McGiffin, recently remembered that his father, Abner, had told him that Uncle John was a very likeable person but a heavy drinker and that he was found dead in a fence corner in Giffin Coulee. He had tried to come home in a severe snowstorm, was bucked off his horse, and fell into the fence corner where he froze to death.

He must have had some years of sobriety and ranching, but his family was surprised to read in *Progressive Men of the State of Montana*[2] a biography in which John was described as "one of the enterprising young farmers and stock raisers who have contributed in a material way to the development of the resources of Cascade County. . . .He came to Great Falls over the Cadout trail making the trip on horseback and being on the road one week. He has a homestead claim of 160 acres with 20 acres under cultivation. . . .He has devoted his attention to raising horses and cattle and has also secured a good yield of grain. His property is valued at $3,500. Mr. McGiffin is a young man of forceful individuality, is straightforward in all his dealings and is worthy of the respect and confidence accorded him."

The Chestnut Valley Roundup where John McGiffin worked as a cowboy was managed by Robert P. Thoroughman[3], who had moved to that valley from Flat Creek on the Mullan Road and near the Dearborn River where he and his wife, Anna, ran the stage station. Thoroughman, along with

Perry Westfall, his wife, Ella, his mother-in-law, Hanoria Considine Berges Cheney, and his daughter, Nora in front of their first Montana home.

John McGiffin, lower left with members of his family in front of homestead home. Nat McGiffin, lower right.

other early-day cattlemen, ran his herds on the open ranges and over a large area. He wrote of experiences on the roundups and in trailing herds of beef to the nearest railroad.

His great-grandson, Richard Thoroughman of Fort Shaw, furnished the following information. The Chestnut Valley Roundup was one of the best known, and a list of some of the other men who were regulars on their crew would include Richard Loss, Toul Allin, John Hodson, Jouett Allin, Alvin Hodson, Bob Chestnut, Bill Birch, Harvey Campbell, Joe and Pratt Wilkinson, Arthur North, and most important of all, Flitch Blackburn, who was in charge of the grub wagon. The outfit had two or three wagons and 30,000 to 40,000 head of cattle.

Thoroughman was often named "Captain" of the roundup crew, and in 1920 Sidney Logan had a letter published in the *Cascade Courier*. He had written it to Bob Thoroughman regarding some of the early-day roundups when Bob was captain and he, Sidney, was a young man just learning the cow business. He wrote: "Your uniform kindness and consideration of the young riders under your charge, your thorough knowledge of the cow business, and permit me to add, your splendid appearance, left upon me a lasting impression of your qualities as the ideal cattleman."

Bob and Anna made the Chestnut Valley their home for the rest of their lives.

Some of those cowboys died with their boots on, and some like Bert Jackson lived to a ripe old age and could describe those open range days to eager listeners.

"That's me holding the horse," he told an interviewer[4] as they looked at a print of Russell's "Bronc to Breakfast" painting. Bert pointed to a young man in the left background holding a horse. "The way I remember it the two here in front are half-breeds. One of them is falling over-backwards trying to get out of the way of that bucking bronc. The way I recall, it happened on the way to the Musselshell about 1887. That morning Russell was sittin' on the grub-wagon taking it all in and sketching it down. The cook was furious with Doc Nelson for trying to ride that bronc and grabbed a butcher knife." Amby Cheney jumped up on the wagon wheel.

Bert Jackson at ninety-seven was chuckling as he related the story. "The horse bucked into the breakfast fire. Knocked the top off the dutch-oven where the biscuits were baking. Spilled the five-gallon can of hot water into the fire. Kicked the frying pan of food into the air. Knocked down the rod holding the big pot of coffee over the fire. Scattered everything.

"Doc Nelson was just a kid. His big brother, Beaver Nelson, was the rep at roundups for George Wilson of the Two Dot spread, H. C. Clark, and others. Doc kept wanting to ride that bronc, but Beaver wouldn't let him. Said he wasn't man enough yet. One morning when Beaver was away Doc tried it, but Beaver was right."

Bert Jackson spent most of his cowboying days working for the '79 Cattle Pool in south-central Montana. John T. Murphy brought in a herd of cattle and established a ranch on Sweet Grass Creek in 1879 and chose that date to be his brand and the name of the ranch, which occupied the area that is now Golden Valley County. In 1887, Murphy brought in two more trail herds from Texas to add to the thousands of cattle he was already running on the open range. There were two, sometimes three, outfits under the '79 brand with headquarters at White Beaver near the present town of Lavina.

Bert worked there and also with Doc Nelson and his brother, Beaver, who was foreman for Two Dot Wilson.

Born Bert Elford Jackson in Bangor, Maine, on March 22, 1874, he came to Montana at the age of five with his parents. His mother turned around and went back to Maine, leaving Bert with his father, who took up a homestead near Martinsdale. Two Dot Wilson took a liking to the boy and wanted to adopt him. That didn't work out but Bert did live with the Wilson family until he was fourteen and old enough to go to work for the '79 Cattle Pool as a horse-wrangler.

In reminiscing many years later, Bert recalled the time when the cowboys who had been on a drinking spree came across a big grizzly bear and decided to rope him. They got the rope around his neck. The bear sat down on his haunches and, paw over paw, pulled the rope, horse, and rider toward him. The rider jumped off his horse, but another man had to shoot the bear to save the horse.

Bert and Charlie Russell worked together for several years as horse wranglers. They always carried 4-H linament for doctoring horses, but sometimes the cook and Charlie mixed it with whiskey for a drink. "It was too hot for me," Bert chuckled again as he told about that.

The camp cooks were usually cantankerous, but Bert remembered this one as being not only cranky but so dirty that the cowboys dragged him down to the Yellowstone River and gave him a bath with a big horse brush and a bar of yellow soap. "Same cook that is in this Bronc to Breakfast picture. He was hoppin' mad but he didn't quit." And the boss didn't even get after the boys for their prank.

During his early years on the range, Bert and another young cowboy got in the middle of a shoot-out in the saloon at Coulson (forerunner of Billings). The boys hid under the bar until the shooting stopped and saved their hides that way.

That didn't scare them nearly as much as the time they were going to hide out in a hay manger and stepped on the bodies of two dead Indians. Some of the '79 cowboys had chased several Indians who had stolen horses from the outfit. They caught up with the Indians; there was a shoot-out and two of the horse thieves were killed and the horses recovered. The cowboys put the bodies of the two dead Indians in the haymow of an old barn, but they had fallen down into the mangers. "I yelled something terrible! Scared me to death!"

Bert recalled one time when he and Russell were in Lewistown and Charlie gambled away not only all his money, but his horse and saddle as well. Bert said he never saw Russell again after he married Nancy.

In 1896, Bert left cowboying, married Anne Cameron, and took up a homestead near present-day Martinsdale. Their daughter, Harriet, was born there but there were no schools and Scottish-born Anne insisted upon a school for her daughter. They moved to Manhattan and Bert worked as an engineer for the Malting Company there. Later they moved to Pony, where Bert engineered a dredge boat and Anne ran a boarding house for the crew. Then for twenty-seven years, Bert was the custodian at the Pony school and Anne boarded the teachers.

Bert died in 1976 at the age of 102 with a century of memories that spanned the open range cattle pool days, the homestead era, the development of mining, and quieter years in the little town of Pony, Montana.

Perry Westfall was born in 1834 in La Harpe, Illinois, and he was to become a prominent cattleman in early-day Montana. Perry didn't start out to be a cowboy; he went West to get rich in the gold fields. As a young man, he watched the wagon trains go by and dreamed of life in the West. Finally, Perry, his brother, and two cousins managed to join one of the wagon trains that was headed for California and the gold rush. They had no horses, no wagon of their own, and no money, so they walked alongside the wagons all the way to California, earning their meals by driving the livestock.

The Westfalls arrived at Sutters Mill in 1851, but by then the big gold rush was over. Along with some other disappointed gold-seekers, they turned around and headed for Placer Gulch in present-day Helena. Walking those many miles was a slow process, and still with no money they had to live off the land. From their hide-out in the brush one day, they saw a wagon train ambushed by Indians, the people killed, and their possessions taken or destroyed. The Westfall boys, by then traveling pretty much alone, decided to travel only at night. This travel in the dark allowed them to avoid both Indians and the intense heat of the desert. As their shoes wore out, they made new ones from pieces of cowhide. When they got to Winnemucca, Nevada, Tom Westfall's feet were so sore that he decided to settle there. He later became sheriff of that county and for many years, the Westfalls were in charge of law enforcement in Winnemucca and the county. Many of Tom's descendents still live in that area.

Perry and his two cousins went on to Montana, where they worked in the placer mines in Helena and in Virginia City. Perry moved to Silver Star and worked in the silver mines there and in the Butte copper mines. He developed a small ranch at Silver Star, which he sold in 1886 when he moved to the Judith Basin. It was the era of the open range and cattle pools. Perry built up a herd, was part of the Judith Basin Pool, and ran his stock on the lush grass of the Judith. He bought the Pete Vann ranch five miles west of the present town of Stanford. He took up additional homesteads, a tree claim, and a desert claim and rented state land to enlarge his own ranges to several thousand acres.

He returned to La Harpe to marry his childhood sweetheart, Ella Berges, and in 1887 brought her to the ranch in Montana. He also brought Ella's thirteen-year-old half-brother, Amby Cheney, with them.

Perry rode with the other owners of cattle in the Judith Basin Pool, and he got Amby a night-herding job with the outfit. Perry was such a big man that, in later years, he did much of his "cowboying" with a team and buggy, riding through his herds and making decisions as to which animals to ship and which to keep. When homesteaders came into the Judith Basin and fenced in the water holes and the formerly open ranges, many of the cattlemen moved their herds across the Missouri River into the Milk River country. Perry, however, chose to keep his cattle in the Judith because he had extensive land holdings and available ranges he could lease.

Ella and Perry built a big house that was the showplace of the area and had the first running water bathroom in the Basin. Eventually they sold the ranch to Melvin and Grace Cheney and moved into Stanford—again to a big modern house. The showpiece there was a piano that had been shipped by riverboat to Fort Benton and freighted to Stanford. It had seven pedals, each one producing the sound of a different musical instrument. Perry was blind during his last years, and he sat in his rocking chair listening to the piano or humming "Over the Waves," dreaming of gold mines, of ranching, and of those herds of cattle that were part of the Judith Basin Cattle Pool.

Gerard Berges was a half-brother to Kid Amby Cheney, and they began homesteading together on Surprise Creek; before that, they had been cowboys for the Judith Basin Pool. In fact, Gerard had been working there for two years before Amby was old enough to get a job.

Gerard helped move several large herds of cattle across the Missouri River to the Bearpaw Mountains and along the Milk River. He was on the posse that chased the last robbers who held up the stage at the Antelope Buttes near Old Stanford. As a Bearpaw Pool cowboy, he was also on the posse that was sent to find Kid Curry after he had shot Pike Landusky.

When Berges quit cowboying, he took up a homestead and then an additional one, a desert claim, and a tree claim. He hired men to work for him and had them take up claims, which he eventually bought. With these claims and isolated quarters of 160 acres, he managed to accumulate some 7,000 acres of owned, isolated, and leased state land. The 400 head of cattle that he owned were "run" like cattle of the open range, getting along on a little wild hay and whatever they could find in his pastures.

Gerard and his family lived quite comfortably on the ranch, but his operation of the cattle business was not very successful, so he tried milking cows and making butter. He churned the cream and put the cold salted butter in their spring house. When he had a wagonload of butter, he took it to Great Falls and tried to sell it door to door. That venture was not successful either.

Berges settled down to being a gentleman rancher and after some thirty years moved with his family to California—nostalgic until his death about Montana and the cattle ranch he once owned there.

They came from Texas, Oklahoma, New Mexico, Kansas, Colorado, Nebraska, Illinois, Arizona, and the Dakotas. They came across the borders from Wyoming and Oregon. Perhaps more cowboys came into Montana from Texas because of the trail herds from that state. But over 90 percent of those trail herd men spent one winter or less in Montana and then headed back for the warmer climate of their home state. Even so, they were an important factor in establishing the cattle industry and the ways of cowboys in Montana.

Modern cowhands and bronc fighters pay homage to those open range cowboys as they wear their customary regalia and improve on it by means of fancy shirts and hats, butterfly boots, bright-colored kerchiefs, and tooled holsters. There are followers of this cowboy tradition not only in the United States but in many parts of the world, as people copy the dress, as little boys play cowboys-and-Indians, and as writers romanticize those early Montana days—the good men and the bad.

This book is an attempt to present the realities of those open range days—who was there and how they lived and worked.

References:
[1] Russell, Charles M., *Trails Plowed Under* (Doubleday & Co., Garden City, NY, 1927) p. 77.
[2] *Progressive Men of the State of Montana* (A. W. Bowen & Co., Chicago, IL, n.d.).
[3]. Letter and information from Richard Thoroughman about his great-grandfather, Robert Thoroughman.
[4] Fenton, Helen B., "That's Me Holding the Horse," article in *Billings Gazette*, reporting an interview with Bert Jackson (n.d.).
[5] Fenton, Helen B., "Jackson, 100, Recalls Russell Painting 'Bronc to Breakfast'," *High Country (News)*, April 10, 1974.
[6] Cheney, Truman, *Ranching in the Shadow of Wolf Butte* (Polebridge Press, Bonner, MT, 1984).

THE COWBOYS' PREACHERS
CHAPTER FIFTEEN

Montana was rough in its early days, and all kinds of people made up its pioneer population. Along with the cowboys and outlaws whose deeds have become legends, there were the preachers. The most famous of those who ministered to the cowboys was Brother Van. William Wesley Van Orsdel was born near Gettysburg, Pennsylvania, in 1848, and because he was the youngest of the family, he was left at home to help on his father's farm while his older brothers fought in the Union Army during the Civil War. After the war, he worked in the western Pennsylvania oil fields, but like the famous Methodist minister, John Wesley, for whom he was named, William was filled with an urge to spread the Gospel of Christ. So he went to Seminary, where he met his future wife. However, when he was twenty-four and she was twenty, she died, and Van Orsdel never remarried.

With missionary zeal, William left home, worked his way on a steam boat up the Missouri River, and landed in Fort Benton. He began his ministry right there. The proprietor of the Four Deuces Saloon was astonished to look up and see a stocky young man wearing a white vest, long black coat, and black Stetson hat standing in the doorway. The young man marched up to the bar, demanding to know where he could hold a preaching service. Without a moment's hesitation, the bartender banged on the bar and announced, "The bar and games will be closed for an hour. Go ahead, preacher." Van Orsdel gulped; it wasn't exactly the kind of place he had visualized holding his first Montana service. He looked over his "congregation" of cowboys, bearded prospectors, and dance hall girls; then he got up on a chair and began to sing in his mellow baritone voice. He was encored again and again, and after a few songs the listeners were interested enough to ask his name. He told them William Wesley Van Orsdel, but they decided it was too complicated and announced that they would just call him "Brother Van."

From Fort Benton he set out for the Blackfoot country to convert the

"Brother Van" William Wesley Van Orsdel, circuit rider for the Methodist Church, was well known and respected by all the cowboys of the open range era. *Photo courtesy of the Montana Historical Society, Helena.*

Indians. When he reached his destination, he found the Catholic priests well established there, and William soon decided that the white men— the cowboys, traders, trappers, miners, and the few settlers east of the Rockies—were more in need of his ministry than the Indians. So he returned to Fort Benton and began his extended work from there—one

Methodist minister in a territory much larger than his native state of Pennsylvania.

There were very few church buildings, so he began his work by preaching in the saloons and occasionally in a schoolhouse in the sparse settlements.

When he entered a saloon and began to sing one of the old Methodist hymns like "When the Roll is Called up Yonder" or "There is a Fountain Filled with Blood," the card playing and the drinking ceased and the rough men around the tables listened in respectful silence. He read from his well-worn Bible and urged them to become Christians in his brief but enthusiastic and powerful sermon.

Brother Van never forgot to "pass the hat" and wonderful were the collections he usually found in it. . .sometimes gold dust in a little sack, sometimes silver dollars, and occasionally a $20 gold piece. Seldom did he find "two-bit" or "four-bit" pieces, as quarters and half-dollars were called in those days. If there were a few poker chips in the hat, the saloon proprietor was always glad to redeem them—often at more than their value.

One Sunday in Utica, the saloon keeper, Long George Grey, announced to his patrons assembled at the bar and card tables, "Fellows, Brother Van is holding a meeting over at the schoolhouse, so I'm going to lock up and you'd all better go over to hear him. I won't keep my saloon open while he's preaching in town." So practically all the cowboys, including Kid Amby and his friends, went. They were good singers and most of them had had a religious upbringing in their homes. Brother Van's sermons filled a need in a lonesome and sometimes very tough land.

No respectable woman was ever found in a saloon in those days so they were happy if there was a schoolhouse for the services. They always prepared bounteous chicken dinners for Brother Van, and he ate as heartily as he preached. He had good reason for that healthy appetite, for he traveled many long miles on horseback or sometimes in a buckboard in order to cover his extensive missionary field. He had to be a good rider with great endurance, and a dependable horse was as vital to him and his work as the cowboy's horse was to him.

One of Charlie Russell's great paintings shows "Brother Van Hunting Buffalo." His long black coat is streaming out behind him and his wide-brimmed hat is jammed down on his head to keep it from blowing off in the wind. Russell gave this painting to the Deaconess Hospital in Great Falls.

Brother Van started his preaching in the saloons, but he soon began to organize churches. Elizabeth McGiffin, who was later to marry Kid Amby Cheney, remembered that as a child of six she heard him preach a powerful sermon to a group made up mostly of rough coal miners from the Stockett-Sand Coulee area. She went home with her mother, firmly resolved that she would never sin again. Seventy years later, she recalled that the text was about the man who built his house on sand and that he had sung a song which he had composed and dedicated to his brother, Tom. "We're Building Three a Day, Dear Tom," meaning three new Methodist churches in Montana.

Brother Van—loved, respected, and influential in early-day Montana—has become a legend, too . . . .a circuit rider who rode horseback to gather in his people, much as the cowboys rode circle to gather in their cattle.

Near the gold camps of Bannack and Virginia City, the first Episcopalian bishop came and eventually founded eleven missions. The work of the Episcopal Church in Montana began when the Rt. Rev. Daniel Sylvester Tuttle arrived in 1867. He was assigned to the mission field of Montana, Idaho, and Utah territories, and his Episcopate covered 316,547 square miles. He had to travel it by horseback or stagecoach. It was the era of bustling mining camps, so most of his work in the earliest years was with those towns and people. Gradually the emphasis changed; cattle were brought into Montana, homesteads were taken up, and pioneers came in covered wagons to claim and work the virgin soil. Deer Lodge was one of Bishop Tuttle's strongest churches, and he soon found cattlemen and cowboys in his congregation as the surrounding area became a stronghold of the cattle industry. His early church in Bozeman was made up of people who were farming the rich Gallatin Valley and trailing in herds of cattle from the Southwest.

Tuttle was followed by the Rt. Rev. Leigh Richmond Brewer, who according to the General Convention, was to be "turned loose in Montana to work in the great Southwest Desert." By then the field had been divided so he had only one territory to cover. Bishop Brewer, a dynamic pioneer churchman, soon set his Eastern colleagues straight that Montana was northern mountain country, not southwest desert, and that he needed more funds and more clergy to carry on the work in this vast area. He was a restless driving man with a great capacity for work, and in his thirty-two years of ministry in Montana, he laid the groundwork for most of the Episcopal churches that exist in the state today.

The first ordained Methodist Episcopal minister in Montana Territory was said to be the Rev. R. M. Craven. He was born in South Carolina in 1848 and fought in the Confederate Army during the Civil War. He arrived in Montana in 1868. His first ministry was in the Prickly Pear Valley near Helena, but in his many years of service in Montana, he preached in widespread areas including the cowboy towns of Utica and Philbrook in Judith Basin Cattle Pool country.

The Rev. Jacob Mills was an early-day minister who came first to Fort Benton, but unlike his predecessors, he had some money and was instrumental in founding the first college in Montana. It was located at Deer Lodge and had two professors—one to teach music and chemistry and the other to teach languages including Latin and Greek. This Montana Collegiate Institute was later merged with Montana Wesleyan to form Intermountain Union College at Helena. After a disastrous earthquake there that destroyed or damaged most of the buildings, the school merged with

Billings Polytechnic to form Rocky Mountain College of Billings. In later years, Kid Amby's daughter and three of his seven sons received their college educations at Intermountain.

There was Francis Asbury Riggin, a well educated gentleman preacher from Pennsylvania, who was sent West for his health and arrived in Montana in the early 1870s. Getting off the train, it was necessary for him to continue his journey by stage. He was wearing a silk top hat such as was the style for gentlemen in the East at that time. The driver of the stage, foreseeing trouble, advised him to wear some other kind of covering for his head, but Riggin was young and stubborn and the driver's well-meant advice was disregarded. All went well until the stage stopped at a station for a meal. A number of cowboys were assembled to greet the arrival of the stage. When they saw Riggin and his hat, they howled in glee—it was just a matter of seconds until they had drawn their guns and the hat was rolling in the dust with a number of bullet holes in it. The young Methodist missionary was a good sport. He took the matter quietly and laughed with the crowd. When the cowboys found out that he was a preacher, they clapped him on the back and chipped in to buy him a new hat, a Western-style Stetson.

Riggin was assigned to work with Van Orsdel, and they made a good team. Riggin was the preacher. He was well-educated, a good sermonizer, and a forceful speaker. Van Orsdel was a singer and an exhorter. He could work the congregation to an emotional pitch that soon brought penitents to the altar. Their circuit was immense in size. Headquarters were in Sheridan; they went down the Jefferson River to Fish Creek and Whitehall, then east to the Tobacco Root Range and Virginia City which was the territorial capital. Farther over the range was the Madison Valley, which was beginning to be filled with settlers and livestock. To the west they journeyed to the valley of the Beaverhead River and beyond it to Bannack and across the Bitterroot Mountains to where Salmon City and Lemhi in Idaho are now.

The Rev. Paul M. Adams was a later Methodist preacher who stayed on in Montana and in 1957 wrote the story of those other pioneer Methodist missionaries in a book called *When Wagon Trails Were Dim*. He begins it with an account: "During my first pastorate in Montana at Virginia City, still a tenderfoot unacquainted with western customs, I went to Sheridan to take some of the Conference examinations. When I boarded the train at 10 p.m. on my return to travel the twenty miles to Alder, the county sheriff, Charles Hill, got off. This was his hometown and he was not going all the way to the county seat. He had been, he told me, to a mining camp at Rochester to pick up a girl, an inhabitant of a brothel, who had been in a fight with another inmate and had struck her on the head with a beer bottle. . . He told me that he had deputized a young man who was going to the county seat to deliver her to the jail. Apparently he wasn't quite satisfied with the arrangement for he asked me to keep an eye on the pair to see that all was right.

"At Alder we transferred to the stage coach for the eleven mile trip up the gulch . . . I sat in the front seat with the driver and the girl and her escort were in the back seat. There was a popular song then 'Only a bird in a gilded cage, a beautiful sight to see.' This she sang, only she modified it to go, 'Only a bird in an iron-bound cage, that's me.' She depicted her downfall with profanities and obscenitites which filled the hours' journey to Virginia City, which we reached about midnight." This was Paul Adams' introduction to Montana. He went on to be an outstanding minister and college professor.

Then there was Gus Hammer, who had come up the trail from Oklahoma with a herd of cattle and worked as a cowboy in the Bearpaw Pool. He could cuss with "mile-long"words and spit tobacco juice farther than most any other cowboy. However, he never drank alcohol and that put him in a class by himself among the cowhands. A group of Bearpaw Pool boys one night, contrary to their usual custom, attended a revival meeting in Chinook. It was led by a Reverend Martin. Gus was there and got converted. After he "got religion," he never swore, smoked, or chewed tobacco. He went back to the roundup camp, rolled up his bed, drew his pay, got on his horse, and rode to Chinook. There he sold his horse and saddle, got on the stagecoach to get to the railroad, and eventually arrived at the Theological Seminary. When he finished his training, he was ordained and came back to Chinook to take a job in the Methodist church there. He also filled pulpits at Browning, Buffalo, Philbrook, Ubet, and Utica.

When Kid Amby's father, Civil War veteran Linas Cheney, died in 1906, the family sent for a minister to conduct the funeral. Hours later, a buggy drove up to the Cheney ranch and the Kid took one look and said, "That's no minister; that's old Gus Hammer."

References:
[1] Adams, Paul M., *When Wagon Trails Were Dim*, Montana Conference Board of Education of the Methodist Church, 1957, pp. 22, 23.
[2] Information from unpublished ms. of Elizabeth McGiffin Cheney, "Good Men and Bad."

THREE OLD MONTANA COWBOYS
CHAPTER SIXTEEN

You wouldn't think of the rich and peaceful Napa Valley in California as a place for three old Montana cowboys to meet, but there they were, Con Price, Kid Amby Cheney, and Billy Rowe sitting in Con's living room that sunny afternoon in 1955.

Cheney was still living in Stanford, Montana, right on the range they had ridden in the early days. He and his wife were traveling in California and had looked up his old friend, Con Price. The spring in his step belied his eighty-one years as he rang the doorbell and was met by a little old stoop-shouldered eighty-seven-year-old man with gray-white hair. Could this be the wild cowboy, that adventurer and rider of many rough strings that had been known throughout the big cattle pools? Amby wondered if this could possibly be the dashing cowboy who had once ridden up to his sweetheart's home leading a saddle horse for a planned elopement? Claudia's father opposed the match, for she was the niece of Governor Toole of Montana and Con was only a wild cowboy. Con remembered that he propped the ladder up to the window and helped her down. They rode away to be married in Great Falls, and now, so many years later, Claudia was serving coffee in their modest California home.

Amby had been taken aback by the appearance of the frail old man, but he asked if this were Con Price's home. "I used to ride on the Basin and Bearpaw pools with him in Montana. My name's Cheney."

"Can't seem to recall anybody named Cheney," Price said, trying hard to think back to those exciting, hard-riding days in Montana.

The caller chuckled, "Do you remember Kid Amby?"

The faded blue eyes lighted up. "Don't tell me you're Kid Amby. I thought they shot him in Lewistown sixty years ago."

The two old fellows clapped each other on the back and threw their arms around each other in pure joy. In his excitement, Con almost forgot to invite the Kid and his wife to "light and set," as the vernacular of the old range days came back into his speech.

Bill Cheney, for many years "Recorder of Marks and Brands" for Montana and his father, Amby Cheney.

By chance, Billy Rowe from Fort Benton came to visit Con on the same afternoon. So after sixty years, here were three old cowboys sitting in upholstered chairs as memories of days in the saddle came tumbling back.

"Con, weren't you one of the Lousy Seven?" Amby asked with a grin, for even in those days the Lousy Seven were dirtier and often drunker than the average hard-living cowhand.

"I sure was and I'll never forget the winter we spent holed up in the cabin in Chinook. It was after one of the last big cattle drives across the Missouri, but we had managed to spend our summer's wages in a week and there we were with no prospect of work until spring."

"Who else was in that bunch, Con?" asked Rowe. "I remember the women in Chinook had to keep their chicken houses locked that winter."

"Yep, we got tired of eating boiled beef, but we did have plenty of that because the Bar R outfit (Stadler and Kaufman) in Helena sent word to Al Molison to butcher a beef to keep us from starving to death. We mighta looked pretty tough but those cattlemen knew they would need us in the spring. Good cowboys were hard to come by."

"Russell was in that bunch, wasn't he?" questioned Amby as he was anxious for more news of his old friends.

"Yes, Charlie Russell and George Barrows, too. Then there was Kid Lowry and Lousy Al Molison, Jim Turnbull, John Thompson, and Tony Crawford. I remember Charlie was the dirtiest one of all. He didn't change his underwear all winter, but all that changed after he met Nancy."

"Darned good cowboys they were," mused Amby, "and I remember when I rode by to see you at Chinook. I was just a kid in those days and the roundup boss, old L. B. Taylor, had hired me to stay out at the main ranch in the Bearpaws to herd the pool's horses away from the Missouri River. Taylor's horses wanted to get back to their homes in the Judith Basin. I had my month's wages in my pocket, and I had intended to send the check to my mother for a Christmas present. You were all so flat broke, I loaned that $40 to you and the men grabbed it up so quick, I didn't have a chance to change my mind. I guess I shouldn't say 'loaned' because I never got it back."

Con chuckled, and Amby went on turning back the pages of history, "You know, I don't have a single scrap of Charlie's pictures, but I guess that's my own fault. Several times when I was riding after cattle down in the Missouri Breaks, I saw pieces of paper stuck on bushes. I usually rode over and got them, but when I saw that they were just another of Russell's sketches, I wadded them up and threw them away. I wish I'd kept some of those drawings as they'd be worth quite a bit of money now."

Bess, who had been quietly listening to the stories, interjected, "We almost got a Russell picture for a wedding present. My father, Nat McGiffin, went to Great Falls to buy a present for us—that was in 1903. He could have bought a Russell painting for $5 but he chose, instead, a copy of a classic European painting of a lady and her daughter picking apples. It cost $15, all beautifully framed, and we still have it."*

They remembered that Russell even admitted that, if he found a good clay bank, he would often stop right there and model a figure. Needless to say, the cattle from his circle wouldn't make it to the branding or shipping herd, so he was happy to be kept on as a horse wrangler, night-herder, and entertainer. Many of the stories he told around the campfires then can now be found in his books, *Rawhide Rawlins* and *Trails Plowed Under*. Later Russell told all these stories to Easterners on the dude ranches, and thus he, with the help of his wife, Nancy, developed a lucrative market for his paintings. The three cowboys kept putting in bits of news about Russell and other mutual long-ago friends.

"Talk about Russell," said Billy Rowe, "Remember the time on Sun Prairie near Malta when the rattlesnake almost got him?

"He was lucky to be alive," said Amby. "I remember that snake story and another close call the time I almost killed him when I pulled an old log off a tumble-down cabin trying to get wood."

* That painting now hangs in the living room of Amby's granddaughter, Karen.

Memories were flooding their minds as the three old men lived again the wild, reckless days before homesteaders and fences ended the open range era. Perhaps Charles Russell was most often in their stories because, with his talent for painting and sculpture as well as story-telling, he had gone on to become famous as he preserved for all time the color, spirit, and actual images of the original cowboys and Indians of Montana. Billy Rowe told of Charlie riding along with the reins wound around the saddle horn; he would take a bit of clay from his pocket and, in a few minutes, mold a replica of his partner mounted on another horse.

Amby recalled how he, Henry Keeton, Charlie Russell, Johnnie Brinkman, Sid Willis, Melve Cheney, and others liked to get together at the old Mint Saloon in Great Falls, have a drink, and talk about the old days when they worked for the Basin and Bearpaw pools. Cheney remembered Russell telling this story: "Up by the Twin Buttes we had to camp for the night and the mosquitoes were so bad that we tied the horses to some trees in the bottom of the coulee. Then to protect them we covered them with tree branches. In the morning we pulled off the branches and those darned mosquitoes had crawled under the branches and eaten the horses, so all we had left was a pile of bones."

The fellows couldn't always get Russell away from his easel and paintings as Nancy felt that Charlie's old range friends led him to the saloons and "dens of iniquity." For this reason, Nancy Russell had very little to do with her husband's cowboy friends or their wives. To the author's mother, Elizabeth McGiffin Cheney, and aunts Grace McGiffin Cheney, Ella Berges Westfall, Lizzie Nihill Berges, and Lena Berges Carthrae, the name of Nancy Russell suggested a person who "high toned" them. The author's father, Kid Amby, had this to say when he was interviewed: "There was one time when Charlie could ride like hell. That was when we came to town to have a few drinks and see the girls. There was nobody in the outfit that could beat Kid Russell to the front door of the hottest place in town."

Billy Rowe came up with his story about the time the outfit was camped south of the Highwoods, and he got so hot and dusty, he took off all his clothes and took a bath in Davis Creek. He got some clean clothes out of his bedroll and decided to wash the dirty ones. He took the rope off his saddle, tied it around the bundle of his underwear, shirt, pants, and socks, and put the whole thing in the ripples of the creek, where the rocks and swift-running water would help wash the dirt out. The next morning the outfit moved camp, and Billy forgot to get his clothes. "I sure did hate to lose that rope."

Clothes weren't very important to cowboys in the early days; a black sateen shirt could be had for 75 cents and work pants averaged one dollar a pair, but no self-respecting cowboy would ride without a decent Stetson hat and good pair of boots. Those high-heeled boots were a symbol and a necessity in the cowboy's life. The heels kept their feet from catching in the stirrup when a bronc threw them off; otherwise many a man would

Con Price—one time rider of the rough-string. He once tried out for the Buffalo Bill Wild West Show. *Photo courtesy of Montana Historical Society, Helena.*

have been dragged to his death.

"In the D.H.S. outfit I worked with as a rep," continued Amby, "eighteen of their thirty cowboys died with their boots on. Some drowned while trying to swim their horses across the Missouri or in crossing on the rotten spring ice on the way to Fort Benton's saloons and women. Others were dragged by their horses; some were shot and died instantly. A few ended up with broken backs when they got thrown or their horse stepped in a badger hole."

"I guess a few of our boys like Ed Starr and Johnny Curry got shot but most of us weren't gunmen or killers though we knew how to use guns when we had to," added Con.

"We were a tough bunch, but we worked hard—sixteen hours a day for $40 a month and grub, and we liked what we were doing," summed up Rowe.

"Never thought Russell would turn out to be the richest and most famous guy in the outfit, but some of the rest did pretty well, too—ended up as ranchers, bankers, and storekeepers." Con was thinking of his friends

Two old cowboys, Amby Cheney and Johnny Brinkman, talk over days on the open range.

from the early days.

"Then there was old Gus Hammer. He turned out to be a preacher. Never would have thought he'd be the one; he could spit tobacco juice farther and cuss louder than any cowboy around," chuckled Amby, "but one night at a revival meeting in Chinook, he really got religion. Ever after that he rode the circuit and was a darn good preacher."

"Maybe we all better start thinkin' along those lines—can't be many more years before we get called to the 'Upper Range,' too," philosophized Con as Amby rose to go.

"We've got to get back to Montana now," Amby said as he shook Con's hand, "and I may not see you again until we both get 'up there' but this talking about the old days brought back a lot of memories."

"Say Kid, don't forget to bring a good rope along with you. I'd still like to learn to lay a loop on a critter's neck or the hind legs the way you did," called Con as he and Billy Rowe watched Amby and his wife get into their car and wave good-bye.

In July of 1964, Kid Amby Cheney passed on to Cowboy Heaven. Many years before that, Con Price, Billy Rowe, and Charlie Russell had gotten "up there."

In Memory of
KID AMBY

I've gone to ride the upper ranges
    And I won't be coming back.
The big Boss up in Heaven
    Said: "Amby, we've a lack
Of top cow hands and wranglers
    Who are handy with a rope,
We've got some cayuse angels
    You'll have to lasso on the lope.
I think you'll like our pastures.
    There's no fences and no barns.
You'll find Russell up here sketchin',
    Price and Hammer spinnin' yarns.
The country's wide and open
    Chuck wagons roll all ways,
Where a man can meet his Maker
    On a range not marked by days.

by Roberta Cheney

References:
[1] Cheney, Elizabeth McGiffin, unpublished manuscript.

B IBLIOGRAPHY

Books:

Abbott, E. C. and Helen Huntington Smith, *We Pointed Them North*, (University of Okla. Press, Norman, 1939).

Abbott, Newton Carl, *Montana in the Making* (Gazette Printing Co., Billings, MT, 1938).

Adams, Andy, *The Log of a Cowboy* (University of Nebraska Press, Lincoln, NE, 1967).

Adams, Paul M., *When Wagon Trails Were Dim* (Mont. Conf. Board of Education, Methodist Church, 1957).

Barker, S. Omar, *Rawhide Rhymes* (Doubleday & Co., Garden City, New York, 1968).

Barrows, John R., *Ubet* (Caxton Printers, Caldwell, ID, 1934).

Brown, Mark H. and W.R. Felton, *Before Barbed Wire* (Bramhall House, New York, 1956).

Burlingame, Merrill G., *A History of Montana* (Lewis Hist. Pub. Co., New York, 1957).

Burlingame, Merrill G., *The Montana Frontier* (State Pub. Co., Helena, 1942).

Cheney, Roberta Carkeek, *Names on the Face of Montana* (Mountain Press, Missoula, MT, 1983).

Cheney, Roberta Carkeek, *Music, Saddles, and Flapjacks, Dudes at the OTO Ranch*, (Mountain Press, Missoula, MT, 1978).

Cheney, Truman M., *Ranching in the Shadow of Wolf Butte* (Polebridge Press, Bonner, MT, 1984).

Coburn, Walt, *Pioneer Cattlemen of Montana, The Story of the Circle C Outfit* (Univ. of Okla. Press, Norman, OK, 1968).

Collier, Ned, ed., *Great Stories of the West* (Doubleday & Co., Garden City, New York, 1971).

Farr, William, and K. Ross Toole, *Montana Images of the Past* (Pruett Pub. Co., Boulder, CO, 1978).

Fletcher, Baylis John, *Up the Trail in '79* (Univ. of Okla. Press, Norman, 1966).

Gressley, Gene M., *Bankers and Cattlemen* (Alfred A. Knopf, New York, 1966).

Hamilton, J.A., *From Wilderness to Statehood, A History of Montana* (Binfords and Mort, Portland, OR, 1957).

Howard, Joseph Kinsey, *Montana High, Wide, and Handsome* (Yale U. Press, New Haven, CT, 1959).

Leakey, John and Nellie Snyder Yost, *The West That Was: From Texas to Montana* (Univ. of Nebraska Press, Lincoln, 1965).

McCracken, Harold, *The Charles M. Russell Book* (Doubleday & Co., Garden City, New York, 1957).

Meagher County, An Early-Day Pictorial History, 1867-1967 (Meagher County News, White Sulphur Springs, MT, 1967).

Mercer, A.S., *Banditti of the Plains* (Univ. of Okla. Press, Norman, 1954).

Phillips, Paul C., ed., *Granville Stuart: Journals and Reminiscences* (Arthur H. Clark Co., Glendale, CA, 1957).

Pioneer Trail's and Trials (Madison County History Association, 1976).

Price, Con, *Memories of Old Montana* (Trail's End Pub. Co., Pasadena, CA, 1945).

Price, Con, *Trails I Rode* (Trail's End Pub. Co., Pasadena, CA, 1947).

Progressive Men of the State of Montana (A. W. Bowen & Co., Chicago, IL, 1900).

Ritch, Johnny, *Horse Feathers* (Naegele Printing Co., Helena, MT, 1940).

Russell, Charles M., *Good Medicine* (Doubleday & Co., Garden City, New York, 1966).

Russell, Charles M., *Trails Plowed Under, Stories of the Old West* (Doubleday & Co., Garden City, New York, 1927).

Sackett, S. J., *Cowboys and the Songs They Sang* (William R. Scott, Inc., New York, 1967).

Sandoz, Mari, *The Cattlemen* (Hastings House, New York, 1958).

South Dakota, Prairie Poets (Lund Press, Minneapolis, MN, 1966).

Toole, K. Ross, *Montana: An Uncommon Land* (Univ. of Okla. Press, Norman, 1959).

Vernam, Glenn R. and Lee M. Rice, *They Saddled the West* (Cornell Maritime Press, Inc., Cambridge, MD, 1975).

Von Richthofen, Walter Baron, *Cattle Raising on the Plains of North America* (Univ. of Okla. Press, Norman, 1964).

Wolcott, Phyllis, *The Saga of Doc Nelson*, pamphlet available from Gallatin County Historical Society, Bozeman, MT, n.d.

Magazines:

Life Magazine

Montana Magazine, Spring 1976, "Kid Curry, Montana Outlaw."

True West, March-April 1962, "Kid Curry and his Brothers," by A. V. Cheney, as told to Mrs. A. V. Cheney.

True West, March-April 1975, "Great Falls' First Black Cowboy," by Roberta C. Cheney.

Newspaper Articles:

Great Falls Tribune, April 9, 1961, "Kid Amby Still Young at 86."
The High Country, April 10, 1974, "Jackson, 100, recalls Russell Painting 'Bronc to Breakfast.' "
Billings Gazette, no date on clipping, "That's Me Holding the Horse," by Helen Fenton from an interview with Bert Jackson.
Billings Gazette, April 28, 1963, "C.M.R. in Music, With Russell Suite."
Judith Basin Press, Stanford, MT, July 23, 1964, "Kid Amby."
"The Man Who Rode 'The Bronc To Breakfast,' " reprint of article sent to the author by Harry Higgins (He didn't know the source).
"A True Story of Cowboy Days," about Kid Amby Cheney, no name of newspaper or date available.
"He Grew Up with the West," (story of Walter Jackson), *Sheridan* [WY] *Press,* October 27, 1973.
Havre Plaindealer, September 30, 1918.

Unpublished manuscripts:

Cheney, Elizabeth, "The Old PN Ferry"
——————————, "The Judith Basin Pool," 1951 (based on interviews with Sid Willis, Johnny Brinkman, Henry Keeton, and Amby and Melvin Cheney).
——————————, "Three Old Cowboys"
——————————, "Good Men and Bad"

Author Truman Cheney and editor Roberta Cheney at their ranch home in Montana.

ABOUT THE AUTHOR

Dr. Truman McGiffin Cheney was born and raised on a cattle ranch in the Judith Basin near Stanford, Montana.

He graduated from Intermountain Union College when it was still in Helena and has graduate degrees from the University of Montana and Oregon State University. His work experience includes teaching and administrative positions in Montana high schools, seven years as State Supervisor of Guidance and Counseling in Montana, teaching at Portland State College and the University of Nevada. For fifteen years, he served as a Counseling and Clinical Psychologist at veterans' hospitals in Fort Meade, South Dakota, and Sheridan, Wyoming.

He is the author of *Ranching in the Shadow of Wolf Butte* and some thirty articles for professional journals in the field of psychology.

His wife, Roberta Carkeek Cheney, has authored several books including *Names on the Face of Montana*. They retired to her original ranch home in the Madison Valley and made their home in the country near Ennis, Montana. Their three children and seven grandchildren have roots that go deep into Montana.

Dr. Truman M. Cheney died in a car accident on April 16, 1990. He was one of the last to know the cowboys of the Open Range, and his recounting here of the stories told to him by his father, Kid Amby, and others is perhaps the most authentic and accurate record of that famous era of Montana history.

Truman spent the last two years of his life researching, remembering, and recording that history. He took the completed manuscript to the publishers only two weeks before he died.